TRAVELING
THE
PRAYER PATHS
OF JESUS

JOHN INDERMARK

UPPER
ROOM BOOKS®
NASHVILLE

Cover design: Bruce Gore/Gore Studio
Cover art: Steven D. Purcell
First printing: 2003

Library of Congress Cataloging-in-Publication

Indermark, John, 1950–
Traveling the Prayer Paths of Jesus / John Indermark.
    p. cm.
ISBN 0-8358-9857-1
1. Jesus Christ—Prayers—Meditations. 2. Prayer—Christianity—Meditations. I. Title.
BV229153 2003
242'.2—dc21   2003004632

Printed in the United States of America

To

GRAM

(Wilhelmina Pfannebecker Cohen)
A woman and grandmother of patient life and steady faith
Who sat and fished with me by the "pond"
Who loved me unconditionally
Who prayed for me
Whom I miss

CONTENTS

FOREWORD

THE DISCIPLINE OF PRAYER forms the cornerstone of
Christian spirituality. We may well envy those first disciples
who had the privilege of moving and resting in the presence
of Christ, listening and watching as he engaged in prayer. Like
them, we yearn for Jesus to "teach us to pray."

Jesus did not teach those disciples or us to pray only in the
example of what has come to be called the Lord's Prayer. The
Gospels provide a surprising breadth of materials that narrate
or refer to occasions when Jesus prayed. The prayers of Jesus,
in words recorded and settings identified, provide a rich and
diverse banquet for those who hunger to pray like Jesus. This
book will guide an encounter with those accounts through
reading, reflection, and exercises of personal spiritual formation, in hopes of deepening your own practice of prayer in
Jesus' example.

Traveling the Prayer Paths of Jesus unfolds in six chapters, and
each explores a setting common to the prayers taken up in that
chapter. The opening chapter (*Out of Solitude*) explores prayers
of Jesus for which we have no words, focusing on how the identified settings may shape our practices of prayer. The second
chapter (*By the Roadside*) takes up individual, recorded prayers
that occur during Jesus' itinerant ministry. The next four chapters look at more extended teachings and times of prayer in
Jesus' life: *On the Mountainside* (Lord's Prayer), *In the Upper Room*
("high priestly" prayer of John 17), *In the Garden* (Gethsemane

prayers), *Upon the Cross* (prayers from the cross). An epilogue contemplates Jesus' final prayers in Emmaus and Bethany in Luke's Gospel. The first reading in each chapter surveys the themes and texts encountered in the remaining six readings.

The structure of *Traveling the Prayer Paths of Jesus* lends itself to a discipline of daily reading and reflection, each chapter consisting of seven readings with accompanying spiritual exercises. You may choose to read one chapter a day or some other variant. If so, please set aside significant time for reflection and the spiritual exercises. The readings rely on the exercises, and vice versa, to move you more deeply into practices of prayer stimulated by Jesus' example. Covering a maximum amount of material in a minimum amount of time will undercut the value of the spiritual formation this work intends to kindle.

Notice that nearly every spiritual exercise suggests a journaling activity. You may be familiar with the discipline of keeping a journal. If so, incorporate that into your experience of this book. If journaling is new to you, try it. You need not be a skilled or polished writer. Journaling records your reflections and thoughts over a period of time. Doing so with *Traveling the Prayer Paths of Jesus* will offer the opportunity to discern movement in your prayer life, as well as the chance to retrieve concerns and issues that might otherwise pass out of mind.

A leader's guide at the end of the book serves as a tool for small groups that wish to use *Traveling the Prayer Paths of Jesus*. While such an experience will add a different dimension to your encounter with this book, the guide is also valuable for individuals. The period of six weeks covered by the six chapters lends itself to this book's use during the season of Lent, a favored time to engage in reflective reading aimed at spiritual growth. However, the readings and disciplines of spiritual formation within this work have been written for use any time in the church year.

Allow the title of this work also to serve as the intent and motive with which you enter every reading and engage in every spiritual exercise. For if we would be "little Christs," the literal meaning of the originally derisive title of Christian bestowed on Jesus' followers long ago, we would do well to travel the prayer paths Jesus set as examples. So enter this book as one who still asks today, "Lord, teach us to pray . . . to pray as Jesus prayed."

ACKNOWLEDGMENTS

JUST AS ONE DOES NOT learn to pray in isolation from others, neither does an author move from concept to manuscript to bound volume without extraordinary help and community along the way. For the past seven years, I have been blessed through the support and encouragement and guidance given me by the staff at Upper Room Books. I believe George Donigian first planted in me the seed of a work on Jesus' prayers. Since then, editors JoAnn Miller and Tony Peterson have helped shepherd this work through proposal on to publication. Rita Collett has done her usual careful work in editing that has sharpened words and syntax, and remained a valued and hospitable friend along with her spouse, the Rev. John Collett.

Over the past two years while working on this project, I have engaged in pastoral ministry on a half-time basis at the United Church of Raymond of Raymond, Washington. I thank the folks there for prayers and interest in my writing. During this same time, I have received significant encouragement and support for my pastoral ministry —and for me as a person—from the Rev. Lynn Longfield, General Presbyter of the Olympia Presbytery, and the Rev. Christine Boardman, interim Conference Minister of the Washington-North Idaho United Church of Christ. Pastors need pastors, and I have benefited greatly from their pastoral ministry.

Twice in this book I have quoted comments made by a friend, writing colleague, and now also retired professor of anthropology and archaeology from Clatsop Community College in Astoria, Oregon, Brian Harrison. I hope you see Brian's depth of thought and spirit in those quotes as I have grown from those same qualities and his friendship over the past several years. My writing continues to bear the positive influence of the members of a writing group I was part of for over ten years: Jenelle Varila, Brian Harrison, Lorne Wirkkala, Pat Thomas, Bob Pyle, Sue Holway, and Greg Darms.

Judy Indermark and Jeff Indermark, wife and son, season my life with love and pride. My writing finds support and inspiration from both of you.

Finally, a word of thanks to a person who gave me one of my greatest compliments in pastoral ministry. A young child named Hillary came to Clatskanie Presbyterian Church in Clatskanie, Oregon, with her grandmother during my interim ministry there. On my last Sunday she handed me a postcard-sized piece of white construction paper. A crayon and pencil landscape colored by her illustrated one side. On the other side, she wrote these words:

> *John, I wish you wouldn't leave us. We'll miss you. You were a good praier and always will be. bie John. Hillary.*

So if you ask what credentials I have for writing a book on prayer, I have to fall back on Hillary's gracious assessment.

Thank you, Hillary!

WEEK ONE

Out of Solitude

Day 1

FORWARD, RETREAT!

LUKE 3:21-22; MARK 1:35; LUKE 5:16;
LUKE 6:12; MARK 6:46; LUKE 9:18

*I*N THE YOUTH PROGRAM at my home church, every fall and spring brought retreats for our two youth groups. The junior youth group went for a day to Camp Mo-Val, while the senior youth group had the privilege of an overnighter there or at another site. Recreation provided a chief component and attraction for both levels. Canoeing or fishing in the small lake and trying to stay up all night in the tents make up most of my memories of retreats at Camp Mo-Val or the Emmaus Home in Marthasville. But not all.

I also remember the importance of discussion times and worship experiences. In particular, I recall one Saturday evening campfire devotional. It was my first year in the senior group, and I had been asked to offer the devotional. Busy with other things, I kept putting off my talk preparation until late Saturday afternoon because I still wasn't sure what I would say. But, with a few notes hastily scribbled just before dinner that I could barely make out by the campfire's light, I managed to stumble my way through the devotional.

Why I even recall giving that devotional is this: It served as the first time I felt a sense of calling to Christian ministry. Other people may speak of a conversion experience, a watershed moment in their life. For me that campfire devotion decisively turned my vocational journey in the direction it would take. I do not think it coincidence that the setting involved a retreat, a time apart from the usual places of life where we all too easily fall into comfortable ruts and favored routines. Christian outdoor ministries experiences can be decisive in a young person's faith and the faith of elders as well. At school and at home, everybody knows you and expects you to conform to predictable patterns. At camp, in retreat, you have the opportunity to see things, and yourself, differently.

The times and places of retreat provide needed components for our growth and change. If you can never get away, it may be difficult to to gain fresh perspectives or renewed energies. Nowhere does the value of retreat find greater affirmation and practice than in the ministry of Jesus.

Prayer serves as a common element in the retreats of Jesus. He intentionally created time and space for the purpose of praying. Of course, it is possible to pray in any and all situations. So why the need for retreat? The answer resides in the meaning of prayer. Countless definitions of prayer abound, but my favorite comes from the catechism of the former German Evangelical church: "Prayer is the conversation of the heart with God."

"Conversation of the heart with God." That conversation is what makes retreat an integral factor in prayer. Retreat allows prayer the quiet and concentration needed to engage the heart in conversation. In the midst of busy lives and constant activity, we may find it difficult to hear the sounds of the heart. When tongues flap and our minds constantly bear a thousand thoughts, the spirit finds little room for still small voices. Prayer and spiritual life need retreat.

Place plays a vital role in the fashioning of retreat and the practice of prayer in solitude. The heart cries out for places where we can *be* quiet and *have* quiet. The spirit thrives in places where we can feel at rest, where we can set aside ordinary responsibilities that take up so much time and energy and allow the heart's conversation to take place. In the scripture texts focused upon in this week's readings, two settings play prominent roles in the retreats of Jesus, mountains and deserted places. Each setting serves the same purpose: to provide striking and humbling experiences of God's presence apart from life's routine.

Seeking regular retreat in and for prayer is a challenging discipline. The challenge resides in the ease with which we find ourselves drawn, spiritually speaking, simply to wing it. We move from one activity to another, from one urgent need to another with scarcely a breath in between for reflection, much less retreat. Viewed individually, each of those activities and needs may be worthwhile and pressing. We neglect the ethical dimension of the gospel and its mandate for action at our peril. Yet the danger of our busyness, even in the best of causes, comes in drained spirits and neglect of the grace that renews. Isaiah 30:15 addresses the nation of Judah, who acts and connives with Egypt to secure her defense against Assyria. In contrast to the attitude that life and future depend entirely on Judah's actions, Isaiah reveals that "in returning and rest you shall be saved; in quietness and in trust shall be your strength." The message for Judah's community of faith holds true for individuals as well. We ignore returning and rest at our own risk: the risk of running on empty, of assuming everything depends on us, of exhausting energies and spirit, of failing to discern God's presence through the fog of activity.

As you read through this week's texts, retreat forms the common thread in Jesus' prayers. It does so, not because teaching, healing, preaching, and feeding are unimportant but because Jesus' prayers in solitude create the context from which his activist ministry proceeds. In modeling our own prayer life in the light of Christ, we take our cue from the solitude he sought for conversation with God: in the dark, upon a mountain, in deserted places. Once we find ourselves in such times and places of retreat, the words will come. The feelings will flow. God's grace will not disappoint us. For "in returning and rest you shall be saved; in quietness and in trust shall be your strength."

Holy God, lead me to solitary places of quiet and rest, where I may see you more clearly, where I may understand how I am seen by you more clearly. And in seeing, may I follow your lead. In Jesus Christ. Amen.

Spiritual Exercise

In your journal, list places of retreat you have known in your life. Reflect on what you have experienced of God and of yourself in those settings. Where can you make the time and space to experience solitude in this coming week, for the sake of prayer that engages the heart in conversation with God?

Day 2

TO BE LOVED

Now when all the people were baptized,
and when Jesus also had been baptized and was praying,
the heaven was opened, and the Holy Spirit descended upon him
in bodily form like a dove. And a voice came from heaven,
"You are my Son, the Beloved; with you I am well pleased."
—Luke 3:21-22

A SET OF PARENTS and sponsors stands on one side of the church chancel. In the arms of one, an infant attired in white wiggles and coos, perhaps wondering what this strange place is. A minister robed in the traditional Geneva gown or servant alb stands on the other side, intoning words and questions that have for generations echoed off church walls. In the midst of those gathered stands a bowl filled with water from a kitchen tap, the same tap used for filling pitchers and soaping lasagna pans and rinsing the hands of servers. A prayer concludes. A voice speaks a name. A hand dips into the bowl, then moistens the brow of the child. Sometimes there is a cry, sometimes only wide eyes. And after comes another prayer.

The scene does not mirror the baptism of Jesus—or does it? The Jordan that day flows with sediment picked up from its long journey from Galilee. Ordinary water used for irrigation and drinking becomes, for an instant at least, the water of life. Ironically, Luke does not narrate the baptism itself. Instead, he begins with Jesus at prayer after the fact. In the solitude Jesus finds after the baptismal waters, he prays.

Luke gives no record of Jesus' prayer: its words, emotions, joys, wonderings. For Luke's Gospel, the exact words of the prayer are not nearly as significant as Jesus' act of prayer. Likewise, our words and thoughts in prayer sometimes take second place to the sheer experience of praying. When we turn our hearts and minds, our spirits and wills to the seeking of God's presence, we may receive what we truly need, whether we realize or vocalize those needs in conscious words or thoughts.

Though we have no clue as to Jesus' words in this prayer following baptism, we do have Luke's testimony as to God's response to that prayer. Heaven opens. Spirit descends. Yet as notable as such wonders are in describing the transformation of this place into holy ground, the key revelation comes in the words of the heavenly voice: "You are my Son, *the Beloved*" (emphasis added). The voice "names" Jesus as the Beloved.

At the outset of public ministry, Jesus knows himself to be loved. Had he prayed for a sign that would assure him of the way to follow, no greater sign could have been given: *You are loved by God.* Everything in Jesus' life flows from this affirmation. Knowing himself loved by God, Jesus can engage in a selfless and prophetic ministry aimed at redemption. The surety of God's love defines Jesus' very identity. When temptation or conflict arises, even when the cross looms large, Jesus can act in absolute trust of that love. Knowing himself loved, Jesus can risk loving.

To open ourselves to God in prayer allows us to experience that same affirmation in our lives. The fundamental word and expression of God's grace comes in the assurance that we are loved by God. God's love of us connects Jesus' baptism to our own, and to the scene of infant baptism that opened this reading. Whenever anyone, infant or elder, comes before the church to receive the gift of the waters, those waters speak and bestow the word: You are loved by God.

The words Jesus prayed after his baptism did not matter to Luke. What did matter was that, in the wake of prayer offered in a time of solitude by the Jordan River's waters, Jesus received his identity as God's Beloved. So God would grace us. The knowledge of God's love for us helps us realize that we need not strive to earn or buy or seize God's love. It is already there, a gift, a part of who we are . . . for we belong to God.

Every time you see the font of baptism in your sanctuary, remember the identity God has bestowed upon you in its waters. Remember you are loved by God.

God of grace, help me to accept your love for me when I feel unworthy or unwanted, when I face challenges that seem overwhelming. And in the knowledge of your love, may I be strengthened by your Spirit to love you and others in return. In Jesus Christ. Amen.

Spiritual Exercise

Recall a time when someone told you he or she loved you. In your journal, write any remembrances you have of what that affirmation stirred in you and how it influenced your life. Read Luke 3:22b aloud, as though spoken by God directly and specifically to you (feel free to substitute "child" or "daughter" for "son" as appropriate). As you read God's affirmation, remember that God declares these same words to you in grace. Offer a prayer of thanksgiving for the knowledge that you are loved by God.

Day 3

WHILE IT WAS STILL VERY DARK

In the morning, while it was still very dark,
[Jesus] got up and went out to a deserted place,
and there he prayed.
—Mark 1:35

*M*OST OF US flee from darkness. A group of us at the
YMCA camp in Potosi, Missouri, had just listened
to one of those awful horror stories that young
adolescent boys love to tell. The gruesome details complete, we
had to walk in the dark from our cabin to the campfire area.
At least we could turn on the porch light that would illumi-
nate a part of the way. We switched the light on, walked out
the door, and started down the steps. Suddenly all went dark.
The light had gone out. No doubt, the escaped homicidal ma-
niac from the story had materialized on our cabin porch. I do
not recall running so fast in my life before or since, and the
others ran right beside me. Though reason should have assured
us of a burned out bulb, the darkness convinced us of mortal
danger. We fled.

Adolescents in the wake of horror stories are not the only
ones who avoid darkness. We may not fear the darkness as did
our ancestors, who kept fires and torches burning all night to
create circles of light and safety from beasts prowling in the
dark. We are more sophisticated than that. We order dusk-to-
dawn halogen lights mounted on power poles from our local
utility district, beacons that flood our yards and those of our
neighbors. We install motion-detector lights on garages so we

can drive into the light rather than the darkness and so any nighttime movement, be it cat burglar or cat, will trigger the sanctuary of light. Darkness threatens our sense of safety. We prefer light.

Yet darkness can be the setting for extraordinary possibilities. Genesis tells us that darkness covered the deep across which the Spirit moved, and from that darkness God spoke creation's birthing words. The Gospel of John reports that Mary Magdalene came to a garden tomb "while it was still dark" and there learned the news that God had been at work in even deeper darkness speaking a new creation's rebirth in Jesus' raising.

In Mark 1:35 we encounter Jesus praying while it "was still very dark." Light can be a distraction, illuminating everything around us. We can lose ourselves while taking in the surrounding vista. In darkness, unless we immerse ourselves in stars, the only other clear place to look is within. The great telescope observatories are built on mountains as far away as possible from sources of "light pollution." And so it may be with prayer. Sometimes prayer seeks out darkness. Such prayer allows us not to be distracted by all that can otherwise capture our minds and hearts and spirits in the light. Such prayer, rather than facilitate escape from the world around us, focuses our attention upon the world, life, and spirit within.

While it was still very dark. Jesus did not always pray in the dark. Darkness did not become the context by which all prayer settings must be measured. It is not a formula Jesus provides for us with here, just one example. We do not lay claim to spiritual superiority by broadcasting personal schedules of daily or weekly disciplines of prayers during the hours of darkness. But on this early morning and a few others, Jesus did seek darkness.

While it was still very dark. With the dark often comes the silence, hinted here by the detail of Jesus' going to a "deserted" place. We need not always go to prayer with community, though perhaps it may be true that one never prays without community in heart or mind. In darkness and silence, prayer may find a tighter focus without the normal distractions that fill our eyes and give us little quiet.

While it was still very dark, [Jesus] . . . prayed. In the middle of night, before others rise, before the sun's light hints its return: pray. Pray in the dark with eyes wide open but with no light to be seen, save that which you discern shining within, where Spirit dwells.

God of night as much as day, Lord of dark as sure as light, lead me to trust you when I cannot see and, in so trusting, to find you in whatever darkness may fall. In Jesus Christ. Amen.

Spiritual Exercise

Recall a vivid experience of darkness. In what ways, if any, did you understand God as part of that experience? Set aside a time this week, tonight if possible, to rise and pray in the dark, not in bed with covers drawn over you but sitting or standing in the dark, perhaps on a porch outdoors. Remove every element of light that you can. Pray, with eyes and spirit open, to God.

Day 4

DESERTED PLACES

But [Jesus] would withdraw to deserted places and pray.
—Luke 5:16

*B*RIAN HARRISON, a friend, anthropologist, and archaeologist, lectured about an archaeological dig in the desert region of Peru known as Cahuachi. His words speak of the power of desert and deserted places.

> *What impresses me most about the desert is that the elements of the universe are reduced to their simplest forms: earth, wind, sun, water. And each is itself simple, entire and whole....And what about my own search for meaning here? What can I take from this place? Two philosophical quotes, from Thoreau and Socrates, respectively: "Simplify, simplify." That is here. This is simple. Sand, wind, sun, water. A bare-bones existence, and even the bones, I can testify, are highly weathered. "The unexamined life is not worth living." That is here too in the attempt to understand the how and why of life twenty centuries ago, and place my own situation in this context. To examine my life here in its simplest form, and consider what I need and want, and the needs and wants of a middle-aged man all that long ago. . . . Each time I come to Cahuachi, I know less about [the ancient peoples of this land], and more about me.*

In the places of which Brian writes and into which Jesus withdrew to pray, support systems disappear. Distractions evaporate. One learns quickly whether the simplicity of existence there will be a welcome relief, an oppressive force—or a bit of both.

The relief afforded in deserted places seems more apparent, at least in the beginning, to those of us who might otherwise find our lives bombarded with activities and responsibilities. The silence and isolation of wilderness offer a buffer from daily burdens. Yet the buffer may quickly hem us in. When the landscape without is stark as far as the eye can see, we may be forced to turn our vision and focus upon a place even more unfamiliar: the terrain within, where we discern what is elemental to life, faith, and existence . . . God.

On more than one occasion Jesus withdrew to deserted places to pray. Perhaps they reminded him of the wilderness experience that launched his ministry. There too life was seen and tempted in its elemental simplicity. Where the tempter sought to redefine life's basic elements as fame and security and a full belly, Jesus discerned the exquisite but taxing simplicity of faithfulness to God in the absence of abundance. Jesus' withdrawal in our verse from Luke contrasts with growing crowds and spreading word. In the face of such mounting pressure, Jesus withdraws. His withdrawal perhaps has less to do with escaping ministry and more to do with seeking the strength to reengage and keep perspective. Simplify, simplify.

The withdrawal to deserted places presents us—*confronts* us—with the need for a clarity of perspective not available when we are crushed by persons and busyness all around. Solitude requires us to take ourselves seriously without all the commotion, all the advice of others about who we are or must be. Solitude invites self-reflection. Deserted places provide a setting where we can be with ourselves and come to be through the One who fashions life using only earth, wind, sun, and water. We need not travel to the coast of Peru or the Judean wilderness to discover such a place. We do need to be willing to cast off distractions, including things of great import, for a time apart. The elemental nature of withdrawal to deserted places can be a means to discover and embrace that which is fundamental to life and faith.

Jesus' seeking of deserted places in his prayer life encourages us to go and pray likewise, taking the setting of such prayer as a cue for its subject. To pray, not seeking grand answers for enigmatic issues that have baffled humankind for centuries but rather to pray for accepting and acting upon life's simplicities. To pray for understanding of what is essential for life and what is peripheral, so that needs and wants do not become confused. To pray for an intense focus that cuts to the heart of what God truly seeks and graciously provides for life.

[Jesus] would withdraw to deserted places and pray. In such places, life reduces to its essential simplicities, and the stark surroundings evoke a focused examination of our own place in the cosmos. Speaking and listening find no distraction, save in the whisperings of spirit with Spirit. Such places may indeed teach us less of them and more about us . . . and more yet about the God who meets us in deserted places.

God of earth and wind, sun and water, you fashion life in the simplest of ways with the simplest of elements. So teach me to listen for life's stirrings in the most basic of places. Amen.

Spiritual Exercise

Sometime this week or season, find a deserted place you will have to yourself for a time of prayer. Do not try to fill the silence with your words and thoughts at every moment. Practice a form of prayer that is as much listening and observing as speaking or thinking. Let the solitude of that place and its elemental nature bring its own lessons to your time there. As possible, make a plan to observe regularly a time of prayer in this place or others like it.

Day 5

IMMERSION

[Jesus] went out to the mountainside to pray;
and he spent the night in prayer to God.
—Luke 6:12, NIV

N-SID-SEN CAMP and Conference Center nestles on the eastern shore of Lake Coeur d'Alene in northern Idaho. It currently serves as a year-round outdoor ministries center for the United Church of Christ. Its name, however, traces to a purpose that predates the arrival of Europeans to this area and perhaps to this continent. In the language of the native people who lived in this area, *n-sid-sen* meant "point of inspiration." Tradition has it that the present site of the church camp approximates the place where young men went alone to spend a night on a vision quest, which revealed to them a sense of identity. Upon returning from this "point of inspiration," they were received as adult members of the tribe. Immersion in the experience of night, away from community, provided the youth a setting in which such inspiration would come.

Immersion. Sometimes in the church we hear the word *immersion* only in reference to a particular baptismal style. Immersion plunges the individual completely under water, as opposed to the sprinkling or even the pouring of water on the head. But immersion carries a far deeper meaning than mere ritual. It suggests a complete absorption in an activity or setting to the point that one may be oblivious to the passage of time or other surrounding events or persons. To the native youth who ventured to *n-sid-sen*, immersion likely involved entering wholly into that place and night and spirit until all else was a blur.

Immersion. What takes your mind and heart from the normal attention to time and schedules and invites you to linger long after others have returned to their routines? Such moments of absorption do not come as much to us in our maturity as they do to children who can play and imagine for hours on end. But when they do occur, they often catch us by surprise and with delight. A day spent in a place of beauty or with a captivating book or alongside an endearing or intriguing person can pass by with little or no awareness of time.

All of which makes this story of Jesus' immersion in prayer at night more fascinating. It is one thing to be immersed in settings of extraordinary grandeur in the day, when eyes and ears can become lost in and entranced by creation's offerings. But what must it be like to be immersed at night, when all that orients us to the outside world is light provided by stars and moon and then only if no clouds pass overhead? In such a setting, the panorama takes shape in the interior life. With so little for the eyes to see, at least compared to the day, the spirit's vision takes center stage. There is a close affinity between Jesus' night in prayer and the vigil kept by those youth at *n-sid-sen*. Both plunge themselves into night, into meditation, in order to seek what (or Whom) will enable them to return enlightened to community presently set aside for the sake of immersion.

Immersion is a difficult spiritual discipline whose chief hurdle may be allowing ourselves opportunity for it. Jesus' praying all night on the mountain might appear to be an unaffordable luxury. We're too busy to do such a thing these days. We have too many responsibilities. Our families couldn't do without us. We carry too much on our shoulders.

If all of this rings true to you, then some experience of

immersion may be precisely what you need. Immersion is not for those who have all the time in the world, who live lives of unlimited leisure. It is for those who carry the weight of the world, who wonder what could possibly come next, who cannot imagine squeezing in another task.

Jesus immersed himself in prayer when there was so much to be done and so little time to do it. Why? Time to nurture the spirit was not, and is not, a secondary luxury to be attended to only after all the *real* work gets done. It *precedes* busyness and routine. Indeed, setting aside time to nurture the spirit can transform busyness and routine into opportunities for faithful living. The question is not whether you can afford to have such times of immersion and inspiration. The question is whether you can afford *not* to have them.

Grant me, O God, a time and place of inspiration. Immerse me in your presence, that I may know you with me in every time and place. In Jesus Christ. Amen.

Spiritual Exercise

Find a place where you will not be disturbed for five minutes. Take two deep breaths and relax. Empty your mind of all else, save an image of a hill beside a lake. Imagine Jesus there, praying. In your mind's eye, place yourself beside Jesus. Listen. He prays for you. He prays your name. Be with Jesus as long as you want. Take a deep breath. Promise to do this exercise again another day, only longer.

Day 6

MOUNTAINS

After saying farewell to them,
[Jesus] went up on the mountain to pray.
—Mark 6:46

MY FAMILY LIVES IN A RIVER VALLEY whose ele-
vation above sea level is barely into the double
digits. The view is largely up and around. Nearby
is a ridge, named Radar after the former early warning radar
station located there that kept vigil during the Cold War. Perhaps a year or two after moving here, we drove the logging
road that twists its way to just below the old station atop
Radar. Trees and forest afforded the main view on the switchbacks leading there. But once we parked and walked the hundred or so yards to the crest, a far different vista unfolded.
Before us stretched the Naselle River emptying into Willapa
Bay—and, beyond, a narrow peninsula of land with threads of
roads and spots of communities separating the bay from the
surf of the Pacific Ocean. Farther and higher were the coastal
mountains of Oregon and to the north, far in the distance, the
Olympic Mountains.

[Jesus] went up on the mountain to pray. We can glean two insights into the place of spiritual retreat from Jesus' choice of
this site. The first has to do with vista, with perspective. View-
ing one's surroundings from a ridge or atop the crest of a
mountain or hill provides sights that engender not only appreciation for creation's beauty but humility for one's place in it.
Those who climb the higher mountains in our region speak of

being awestruck at the view afforded them. So it is with places of spiritual retreat. If they provide us with a striking and humbling perspective on our lives in the hands of God, they fulfill their purpose. We have climbed the mountain with Jesus.

A second insight into the meaning of place for our spiritual retreats is found in the great lengths to which Jesus went to secure such places of retreat. Ascending the mountains of Galilee and Judea is no different from other mountain ascents. The way is uphill. Switchbacks make us question whether the trip is worth it. Finding our places of retreat may pose similar problems for us. The way may seem uphill when so many other pressing and practical matters demand our time. The switchbacks of adjusting schedules and setting priorities to allow room for retreat, which often means saying no to other demands, may cause us to question the necessity of such a discipline.

And it is a discipline, to that I can testify. In twenty-five years of ordained ministry, I do not recall a Sunday when I have stood before a congregation and said, "Well, this was a tough week, so I don't have a sermon for you." But in those same years of ministry, the setting apart of time for regular retreat in prayer has been perhaps the hardest calling of my spiritual life. Why? Because it is so easy to tend to the busyness that swallows my time, as I am sure it is for you. We have been raised to be activists in the faith and for good reason. But action without reflection drains us, leaving us with perspectives no broader or higher than the thickening hedge of dates, meetings, and appointments that fill our calendars and handheld databanks.

The temptation in busy times is to press ahead. Prayer and renewal will have to be caught up with later when we have more time. Postponing a retreat often seems the easier thing to do, but it is also the exhausting one—far more exhausting than trudging up switchback after switchback in search of a clearer view, a broader perspective, an experience of renewal.

Jesus beckons us upward. Those who climb the high places often find piles of rocks called cairns left behind as memorials of others who passed this way, and sometimes left to serve as landmarks for the ascent of others. When we venture toward those high places that bring perspective and renewal to our spirits, we find similar landmarks and memorials that orient us to the path we take. Mark 6:46 is a such a cairn. As we make our spiritual ascents, difficult though they may be, we learn why Christ made the ascent before us. Christ's presence opens our eyes to the vista we will discover on the mountain.

Holy God, draw me to high places whose vistas reveal the paths and intersections of life, as it is and can be, with you. Lead me to those high places, and go with me as I leave them to serve you and others in the valleys below. In Jesus Christ. Amen.

Spiritual Exercise

Go to a high place that provides a vista: a second-story window, a hill or knoll in a park, a high-rise viewpoint. Take in all the sights and signs of life you see below. Imagine now that you are looking down on the events and relationships in your life with such a clear and encompassing perspective. Where in your life do you see God? Where in your life do you long to have God? Write down those thoughts in your journal. Pray for God's presence to journey with you.

Day 7

WHEN QUESTIONS COME

*Once when Jesus was praying alone,
with only the disciples near him, he asked them. . . .*
—Luke 9:18

*H*AVE YOU ever felt alone while surrounded by others? The Gospel of Luke turns a curious phrase here: Jesus prays *alone* with the disciples near him. Clearly, Jesus is not alone in the sense of being unaccompanied. The disciples are there with him. So perhaps this verse refers to Jesus' engaging in prayer by himself while the disciples do whatever it is disciples do when Jesus enters prayer: stay out of his way; keep the conversation level down to a dull roar; wonder why, or how, the Teacher can somehow be alone in prayer in the midst of them.

But if Luke's phrase seems curious, prepare for yet another sharp turn in the text: When Jesus prays alone with the disciples near, *he asks them.* The text does not say he raises the question at the conclusion of prayer. While he prays, the question comes.

Most of us pray for answers. We face some decision or crisis in life, the way ahead unclear. We long for guidance and pray for an answer. "God answers prayers" is the byword and assurance that guides our approach to the throne in prayer, and we bring our intercessions before the One who hears us even before we speak or think.

But for Jesus, in this instance, prayer evokes questions.

I have experienced times in my prayer life when mind and

spirit seemed more awash in questions rather than answers. More than once I have taken those times as indicators that I was not praying "right" or with a proper spirit. If only I could trust more, or if only I could clear out whatever in me was forming these questions. But many times, if not most, questions do not arise from our weakness nor do they signal bad faith. They arise simply from the events that lead us to prayer. Some questions come from the heart of God speaking to our hearts. Questions have regularly filled my prayers of late: Why should the six-month-old daughter of friends have a tumor on her brain, or why should the young wife whose marriage I presided over barely a year ago be widowed two days after the birth of her first child, or why _____ ? I leave it to you to fill in the blank with questions that have intruded into your prayers.

What we *do* with the questions that arise in prayer is our challenge. To deny them, to cut them off, to submerge them deep inside in the hope they will just "go away" offers one set of response. But such a response will likely only delay and fester whatever generates such wonderings. And what if the questions we feel rising inside are, in fact, the *answers* God has for us at the moment? We do not know the words and thoughts of Jesus' prayer that evoked his question of the disciples. We read too much into the text to say the question came to him directly out of prayer as the word God gave. On the other hand, we treat the text too lightly not to discern that, for Luke and for those disciples, there was a close though unspoken connection between Jesus at prayer and his questioning of the disciples on the matter of his identity.

When Jesus was praying alone . . . he asked them.

Questions that come in prayer call for expression and invite reflection. They stir in us new possibilities, even if for the moment they bewilder us with uncertainties. Luke's narrative portrays a fascinating link between prayer and question; we do not know the prayer, but we do know the question it apparently evoked. Individuals and communities of faith can benefit from the lesson afforded in Jesus' example: When questions arise, bring them forward.

In moments of private devotion, the presence of questions may seem to imply bad faith on our part, making us feel as if we alone are the only ones who have ever had this experience. In reality, the questions may be God's way of pushing us toward deeper faith and into community with other seekers who wrestle (or *need* to wrestle) with what troubles.

Give ear to my heart, O God, when I come to you in prayer. Grant me guidance and holy presence, even if for the moment that urging and accompanying take the form of a question. May I receive your grace in whatever form it takes. In Jesus Christ. Amen.

Spiritual Exercise

Begin to keep notes or journal any question(s) that you experience in your prayers. Over the course of a week or longer, reflect not only on where or why those questions arise, but what they might have in common. How might these questions and their shared themes or concerns represent a word God brings to you? Consider sharing these thoughts with your pastor or a trusted spiritual friend.

WEEK TWO

By the Roadside

Day One

THE JOURNEY IS OUR HOME

MATTHEW 19:13; JOHN 6:11; MARK 9:29;
LUKE 10:21; JOHN 11:41-43; LUKE 9:29, 35

*R*OAD TRIPS. WHEN I was a child traveling with my family, the destinations were everything: a motel with a swimming pool at the end of a long, hot drive; the sight of aunt and uncle and cousins not seen since the prior summer; the farmhouse and its pond and climbing trees. Getting there, the journey, was more of a chore. We pulled out games or invented them to pass the time. When all else failed, I stared at clouds to decipher some giant, some city, formed of streaking cirrus or white cumulus or gray-green thunderheads. All manner of scenes and life passed unobserved. The journey merely served as a means to an end.

Since then I have learned to value the gift of journey for its own sake. Part of that appreciation has come in sights seen and experiences gained along the way that have not necessarily related to final destinations. Part of that appreciation has come in an awakening to life itself as journey and spiritual pilgrimage.

The metaphor linking journey to faith traces back to our most ancient sacred writings. In the Psalms we encounter songs lifted by those who made pilgrimage to Jerusalem. "I was glad when they said to me, 'Let us go to the house of the LORD!'... Jerusalem—built as a city that is bound firmly together. To it the tribes go up" (Ps. 122:1, 3-4). Even more distant in time,

Israel's wilderness sojourn narrates a story of faith (and unfaith) and journey inextricably meshed.

The Gospels' telling of Jesus' life and ministry is not a sedentary tale. Jesus does not set up shop in Nazareth or Jerusalem, posting office hours when he may be available, waiting to be found. The first half of Mark's Gospel especially captures the vagrant nature of Jesus' ministry out and about in the world. Now he is in Galilee, next he crosses its sea, then to the north, and again to the south. Only when Jerusalem and suffering and cross come clearly into view does destination take precedence.

Until then, Jesus' ministry is all journey. But it is not helter-skelter, rushing to get from here to there with no pause to consider what or who lies between the day's beginning and its ending. The Gospels' narrations dwell on the journey's "scenery." Matthew 9:35-38 provides this crucial insight into Jesus' weaving of ministry and journey in one common cloth:

> *Then Jesus went about all the cities and villages, teaching in their synagogues, and proclaiming the good news of the kingdom, and curing every disease and every sickness. When he saw the crowds, he had compassion for them, because they were harassed and helpless, like sheep without a shepherd. Then he said to his disciples, "The harvest is plentiful, but the laborers are few; therefore ask the Lord of the harvest to send out laborers into his harvest."*

It is not Capernaum or Nazareth, Caesarea Philippi or Bethsaida that provides the starred attractions toward which all is directed. No, it is the people encountered along the way in scenes of extraordinary beauty, in settings of poverty, in places where illness and death loom. Jesus' journey and ministry are not consumed by the press of getting from here to there. Journey and ministry focus on passing scenes and persons no longer passed by but attended by a presence willing to be distracted by life.

Along the road, we find Jesus at prayer, but not in roadside chapels, white clapboard sanctuaries intended to draw attention to themselves. As with the journey itself, Jesus prays in those places and with those persons who might otherwise be seen as diversions and distractions from the "real" destination: with children whose caretakers risk censure for seeking a hand and prayer upon a little one; with a crowd hungering for food and hope, even as disciples wonder where either might be found; in the face of evil; in the presence of a loved one's death. By the roadside, throughout the journey, Jesus prays.

Pilgrimage continues to be an important metaphor for spiritual growth as it communicates our very identity as persons and communities of faith. Jesus' ministry found its most frequent context and practice on the journey. Gospel and movement go hand in hand. The roots of Jesus tapped into the presence of God underlying life, not just into particular places or traditions or expectations. His prayers took into account the changing scenes and persons encountered along the way. Jesus did not presume one setting for prayer, be it synagogue, Temple, or prayer closet. The discipline of prayer followed and entered the whole of life.

Our prayer life relies on the "interior" life, on moments of solitude away and apart. The first chapter of this book underscored that need. But spirituality is not exhausted in the private prayer closet. We carry our experience of God's presence and our conversation with the heart of God into the places where we conduct our business, raise our families, enjoy our leisure, engage in social and political involvements, and refresh ourselves in friendships. All of those relationships require journeys outside the cocoon of solitary life. We venture out to be with others, to be for others.

For some, clear and pressing goals drive those journeys. We may well set out clearly defined "destinations" for career and family and community. Such goals can indeed lend a sense of urgency and clarity to our lives. But in getting from here to there, we must not neglect what or whom we will come upon along the way. Our prayer life is more than striving for premeditated goals and arriving at anticipated destinations: the discipline of prayer invites us to practice, as Jesus practiced, a sensitivity and compassion for those persons and needs encountered on the way.

Allow the readings of this week in particular to urge you toward a spirituality open not only to opportunities for prayerful ministry upon your journey but to opportunities to experience the very presence of God in those persons and places you might otherwise overlook as distractions.

Holy God, as you guide my steps, so also guide my eyes and ears that I may not be so busy with my priorities as to miss the priority of seeing and ministering to you. In Jesus Christ. Amen.

Spiritual Exercise

Consider your normal routines in a day. In your journal, reflect upon the purposes those routines serve. Set aside one time each day for prayer that intentionally considers how that day's routine has been changed by someone or some need encountered on your journey. How has that experience brought you into deeper awareness of God's presence?

Day Two

INTERRUPTIONS

*Then little children were being brought to [Jesus] in order that
he might lay his hands on them and pray.*
—Matthew 19:13

*M*Y HOME CHURCH pastor told a story shortly after
he had taken a tour group to the Holy Land. Years
later I found the detail he described in a volume
from 1912 entitled *A Camera Crusade through the Holy Land*. It
regards the Church of the Nativity in Bethlehem, built over
the traditional site of Jesus' birth. Some say it is the most ancient Christian church in the world. But its age is not the story.
Its doorway is.

An ancient gray wall faces the street with a solitary portal
leading into the church. The outline of a far higher and wider
door can be seen in the pattern created by newer bricks that
lowered and narrowed the older entry. As a result, the present
doorway is accessible only to those who stoop as low, you
could say, as a child. The reason for the door's diminished size
dates back to the Crusades when men of war rode into
churches on horseback to worship, pillage, or stable their ani-
mals. So pious keepers of the Church of the Nativity bricked
in this doorway to eliminate any possibility of entry on horseback—a practical move, no doubt, but one also charged with
good theology. For the door to the Bethlehem church embodies a stark symbol of Jesus' teaching about God's kingdom
and our posturing. Unless we become as a child, we cannot
enter either that church or that kingdom.

Then little children were being brought to him in order that he might lay his hands on them and pray. The disciples spoke sternly to those who brought them. . . . These disciples aren't bad or evil persons. They just know about priorities. Imagine their thoughts when this parade of runny-nosed toddlers and grimy-faced tykes starts closing ranks round the rabbi: *There are sermons to be preached, diseased people to be cured. And didn't the Master just speak of Jerusalem and suffering? So much to do, and so little time. Go on, shoo! Don't bother the rabbi. He's too busy, too important!* And the disciples have a point. Matthew declares up front that people have brought these children to Jesus for no big reason. All they desire from Jesus are his touch and prayers for the little ones. You don't have to be God's gift to humanity to touch children or pray for them. Anybody can do that. People with less important things to do can do that. Don't bother the rabbi! Don't interrupt *his* ministry.

But as one of my preaching mentors once said, interruptions often *are* the ministry: the phone call in the midst of sermon preparation, the drop-in visit at the office, all the unscheduled moments when matters we thought important enough to block out time on the calendar for are met with opportunities to respond to another human being. Now here's the catch. Life and ministry don't work that way just for ordained ministers. God splatters *each* of our lives with unheralded yet opportune moments that come at us out of nowhere. And we're left to decide in that figurative or literal split second: What and who is more important?

Jesus' indignation toward the disciples arises from his unspoken determination that these children are just as important as sermons and parables and Pharisees. He makes time and space for the little ones to come to him, remarking in the process that the disciples could learn a thing or two from them about God's kingdom. In Jesus' example, we see how we can

respond to little ones today, whether they be little in age, pres-
tige, power, or money. What do we do, whom do we choose,
for whom do we pray, when our busy-ness encounters persons
whom others belittle as insignificant interruptions?

The prayers of Jesus by the roadside begin with a group of
children not on the day's agenda. But for those considered by
others to be an unwelcome imposition, Jesus bends down low.
The door to the church at Bethlehem finds its model for mea-
surement and humility in Jesus' touching of these children. May
our prayers likewise be moved to include the unexpected interruptions in our lives in order to touch the needs of God's
children.

*God of the child, Lord of every moment, expected or not, open my
prayers and heart to the unexpected ways in which you come to me.
Allow me to be surprised and distracted into ministry and prayer that
touches the lives of your children. In Jesus Christ. Amen.*

Spiritual Exercise

Practice a stretching exercise of prayer. Lower your body as
you are able, bowing down, kneeling, or lowering your head.
Call to mind and heart a person or group bent down by life or
small in comparison to what they face. Pray for that individual
or group from your own lowered posture. As you rise up from
prayer, imagine lifting them up with you. Pray for God so to
lift them.

Day 3

TABLE BLESSINGS

Then Jesus took the loaves,
and when he had given thanks,
he distributed them to those who were seated;
so also the fish, as much as they wanted.
—John 6:11

*C*OME, LORD JESUS, *be our guest; and let this food to us be blessed.* Table prayers, along with bedtime prayers, form some of our earliest remembrances and practices of prayer. To be sure, they risk degenerating into rote habit, uttered practically without thinking. On the other hand, table prayers possess the potential of connective ritual, linking our experience of sustenance in the meal to the balance of food, relationship, and grace that nourishes us into wholeness. Indeed, we speak of such prayers as "saying grace"—a reminder that breaking bread, whether our board be set in sanctuary or homeless shelter, living room or refugee camp, may serve as a sign and embodiment of God's providential care.

Jesus offers a table blessing in John 6, though the table is by no means typical in its company or its feast. Family does not comprise the table mates. No carefully crafted guest list exists to insure the balance of friends and "right" people. No, a crowd tags along behind Jesus. John declares that the crowd had seen what he had done for the sick elsewhere, perhaps a mixed crew of beggars and those with physical disabilities and others at wit's end, desperate enough in their circumstances to follow any hope of cure, healing, or release. Even climbing up a mountain does not give Jesus respite from those who want or need more.

Jesus and the crowd meet at a table, albeit an unusual one. This table has no polished wooden surface. No chairs fringe its dimensions. No candles burn; no silver service glistens. In truth, the table takes shape in two human hands holding loaves blessed in a human prayer of thanksgiving.

Neither John nor the other Gospel writers record Jesus' actual words of thanks and blessing. As a devout Jew, Jesus would have regularly offered table blessings to God the Creator, God the giver of manna in the wilderness, God the Lord of vine and grain. But whether the words intoned ring familiar or spring new, Jesus' blessing fashions that day's table. The words of God's bounties feed spirits and then stomachs. Who is to say which is the greater miracle?

Jesus prayed the table into being, and all were fed as a result. Perhaps we get things out of order in our table prayers at times. We plan and prepare and fuss to make sure the table is ready and full, and only then do we pray in gratitude for what we see and smell, knowing what we will soon touch and taste. Jesus' blessing created the table, giving thanks for what less discerning eyes would have rightfully judged grossly inadequate to the needs of five thousand. What does it mean to you that Jesus gives thanks before abundance is apparent? What does it mean to the church that Jesus gives thanks without an overflowing larder already set?

Individuals and communities of faith would do well to consider those questions. Most who read this book live in a society and community of material abundance. We do not sit before empty tables and say grace when it seems there cannot possibly be enough to go around. We do not gather in sanctuaries, dark and cold from a lack of resources to pay for energy costs. We may be apt to congratulate ourselves and our hard work for the bountiful tables we enjoy and to imagine the abundance is what generates (or is required for) prayerful thanks.

Jesus prays the other way around. In scarcity Jesus gives thanks . . . and all are fed. Abundance, or at least what is sufficient for the day, follows thanks. The table that sustains us originates not in what we bring to it but in God's providential care that sets the board and makes the feast.

Jesus trusts God. Out of that trust, five loaves and two fish in the face of five thousand become cause for thanksgiving.

I guess that's why they call it "saying grace."

Give us this day our daily bread. For that gift from your hand, Lord Jesus, may I be thankful, and may I share with thanksgiving. Amen.

Spiritual Exercise

The next meal you prepare, offer a prayer of thanks *before* you prepare it. Offer words of gratitude to God for the gift of food and access to it. Be mindful of those whose hands picked fruit or vegetables, prepared meat, baked bread, or packed boxes you will use. As you prepare the meal, pray for those who will share it with you at table. Fix an extra portion or two for a neighbor or friend for whom it might be a welcome gift. If possible, arrange to serve a meal at a shelter. In all these things, give thanks to God.

Day 4

PRAYER AND EVIL

"This kind can come out only through prayer."
—Mark 9:29

*I*T'S OUT OF MY HANDS now. I can't do anymore." The words may find voice in any number of situations. A physician meets with the parents of a child wracked with fever and infection. Everything that can be done medically has been done. Whether healing comes remains to be seen. Or the words may be spoken by a friend or spouse whose repeated attempts to dissuade the other from destructive behavior have gone unheeded, and a breaking point has been reached.

Lines do get crossed. Situations do arise when our personal interventions and resources run out, and we can do no more.

Jesus' words in Mark 9:29 carry an edge of disappointment toward the disciples' failure to help a child suffering from an affliction. But Jesus' words also hint at the realization that we do not possess within ourselves the means to resolve every need or conflict we face. Self-reliance is not the ultimate Christian virtue. Faith pushes us to recognize that some resolutions finally reside beyond us. For those resolutions, we can only intercede in prayer to God. We remain open to doing what we can do, committed to serving as God's instrument in response. But in the end we pray, understanding that the problem is bigger than we are.

This truth of ultimate reliance on and trust in God comes to the forefront in the presence of evil.

In Mark's narrative, evil in terms of the consequences of this child's affliction threatens his life: "'It has often cast him into the fire and into the water, to destroy him'" (9:22). Why this child, this innocent, has been stricken the text does not even begin to address. Speculation over such matters is a luxury of the uninvolved, who see no need to confront injustice. Jesus' intervention aims not for greater understanding of a philosophical dilemma but for the release, healing, and restoration of a child to family, community, and wholeness.

This kind can come out only through prayer. Jesus directs the disciples, and us with them, to a reliance upon God and not self alone. We work and minister in the face of evil as best we can, but at times we reach our limits. What if finding a just solution acceptable to Israelis and Palestinians in ending the evils wrought by both sides depended only on human reason and effort? We need not reach so far as that to understand the dilemma acknowledged—and the hope proposed—in Mark 9:29. Domestic partners fall into a cycle of distrust, where each succeeding disappointment sours the relationship until it seems irretrievably broken. Gossip in the church subverts community until partisan patterns of communication harden into uncritical praise of those friendly to a given agenda and unrelenting sniping at those who are not. Evil need not take extreme form, as in persons willing to fly loaded passenger planes into buildings. Evil has its day whenever truth, community, and compassion fall victim to ignorance, prerogative, and self-interest.

This kind can come out only through prayer. Left to ourselves and our resources alone, hope might seem ludicrous. We seem too close to, if not part of, the problem. Attitudes have been set for too many years, if not generations, to flex or change or renew.

But we do not live to ourselves alone, nor does God abandon us to ourselves alone. Prayer connects us to the One whose knowledge of evil is not secondhand or speculative. In the cross, God took upon and into God's own self the power of evil to do its worst. God's raising of Jesus revealed evil's limits.

God gives capabilities for work, ministry, and service that we are to exercise to their utmost. But when we reach our limits, particularly in the face of evil, prayer connects us to the One whose suffering in Jesus Crucified becomes hope through Christ Risen. Evil does not have the final word. Life does.

Deliver us from evil, your Son taught us. Holy God, deliver me—not by denial of evil, not by silence in its face, not by removing my earnest wrestling with it. Deliver me when I can do no more. And when I can do no more, move me to pray more and trust more, finding fresh energy and faith to be your servant engaged for new ministry. Amen.

Spiritual Exercise

In your journal or diary, write down several places or relationships in your life where you know you cannot go it alone or where you have reached your limits. Intentionally pray today and in the coming days about each of those situations. Offer them to God, not as an act of resignation but as one of trust. Pray for God's intervention in you, in others, and for the good, without limiting God as to what the "good" will be. Trust. Listen. Expect. Hope. Wait. Serve.

Day 5

SPIRITED PRAYER

*At that same hour Jesus rejoiced in the Holy Spirit and said,
"I thank you, Father, Lord of heaven and earth. . . . "*
—Luke 10:21

*H*AVE YOU EVER FOUND yourself overwhelmed by joy?
Have you ever found yourself overwhelmed by joy
that moved you to lose yourself in praise?

I remember attending an evening service of a Catholic
charismatic community while I was in college. Some friends
from my home church were active in the charismatic renewal
movement, and I had attended prayer groups in which they
were involved. So I knew what might be expected at that
evening service in terms of speaking in tongues or "prophesy-
ing." What caught me totally unprepared was the beauty and
surprise of an experience later described to me as "singing" in
tongues. One person's voice began intoning a language and
melody I did not recognize. Then another voice joined in and
then another, until gradually what seemed to be fifteen or
more voices wove in and out of a harmonic form that defies
clear description. My experience of the music suggested an
extraordinary spontaneity in praise led by God's spirit.

We need not be charismatic to lose ourselves in praise and
wonder. But we do need a willingness to be struck by awe or
surprised by the gift or realization of joy. In prim and proper
theologies (not to mention liturgies) of "a place for everything
and everything in its place," we sometimes deny God's spirit
the opportunity to run chills up and down our spine or let

loose with a spontaneous offering of praise or thanksgiving in a time and place not planned and packaged as such.

Jesus allows himself the gift of responding with spontaneous joy in this simple prayer of thanksgiving. There is no need to wait for the arrival of sabbath or synagogue or prayer cubicle. The news brought by the seventy returning from a mission commanded by Jesus, a return not coincidentally described by Luke as "with joy" (Luke 10:17*a*), moves Jesus to rejoice then and there in the Holy Spirit and to pray with thanksgiving for God's surprising choices in life. Joy can be infectious. Prayer can be spontaneous. So Jesus demonstrates by the roadside.

Forming our lives and prayers in the example of Christ may benefit from supportive regimens and disciplines. But spiritual formation that does not encourage spontaneity and surprise, wonder and awe, can transform those disciplines into empty shells where everything must fit into preconceived and institutionally approved habits learned by rote rather than by heart.

The very content of Jesus' prayer hints at the sometimes subversive ways of God: "I thank you . . . because you have hidden these things from the wise and the intelligent and have revealed them to infants" (Luke 10:21). The ability to be surprised, the openness to being swept up in praise, suggests a certain acceptance of our inability to know all the answers and a willingness occasionally to let go of our tendency to control things. Jesus seeks a vulnerability not to that which will harm us but to the Spirit who will bring deeper freedom to our lives and greater openness to discerning the call and joy of God in experiences not calculated or expected.

At that same hour Jesus rejoiced in the Holy Spirit. We need not delay joy and the prayer and thanksgiving that accompany it until scheduled gatherings or formal liturgies. Our prayers, and with them our spirits, find themselves formed whenever we respond to the intersection of our lives with grace. Like Jesus, we can stop midstride, midsentence, when our eyes or ears or spirits perceive that we stand on holy ground. At any place. In any time. Rejoice in the Holy Spirit . . . and give thanks.

I thank you, O God, for every turn of life that brings the quietest hint or loudest shout of your love's presence and working. Help me to offer thanks more timely to their causes. Amen.

Spiritual Exercise

When was the last time you found yourself overwhelmed by the desire or need to offer a prayer of thanksgiving? How and when did you respond? How did your response compare to the usual "time lag" between more ordinary experiences for which you are grateful to God and your prayers of thanks? Resolve to lessen the time between the experience and the thanksgiving. Begin today by offering a silent or verbal prayer for the next experience that moves you toward thanksgiving. Think of this process as breathing: When a cause of thanks comes, it is the breath you receive; when you offer thanks, it is the breath you return.

Day 6

PRAYERS AND HEARING

And Jesus looked upward and said, "Father, I thank you
for having heard me. I knew that you always hear me,
but I have said this for the sake of the crowd standing here . . . "
When he had said this, he cried out with a loud voice,
"Lazarus, come out!"

—John 11:41-43

OD HEARS OUR PRAYERS. I once heard a news account
of a six-year-old child ravaged by a rare disease that
caused an extreme brittleness in his bones. In the
course of his young lifetime, the child had endured more than
fifty operations as a result of having suffered over two hundred
broken bones. One wonders how to speak of God's hearing
the prayers of that child and his parents.

Prayer moves us into a realm of mystery not easily summa-
rized in pat answers. We may approach prayer as we would a
supermarket, with a shopping list of needs and wants firmly in
hand and clearly in mind. Or we may practice prayer as a
means of weighing in deity in our corner, whether for our side
of an argument . . . or our side in a war. God will hear us no
matter what we say, so the reasoning goes, so let's invoke God's
help in finding the lost car keys.

In the face of such suffocating certainties about prayer, I
sometimes prefer the company of those who wrestle with
what it is we do in prayer and why. These folks ask, If God
knows our deepest and innermost thoughts, why do we need
to pray? My anthropologist friend, whom I introduced in the

last chapter, offered such musings in his insightful reflection on prayer.

> *I know prayer can be tremendously comforting, and that in it-self is enough. I am able to pray for the safety of my friends, even if I am not certain to whom I am praying, or of the result. It reduces anxiety if you can hand off responsibility for life and death, not to mention life after death, to a supreme being. But I don't know if it is efficacious. Maybe there is some karmic ledger kept, but it's hard to imagine God as a supercomputer keeping track of how many prayers have been received in favor of the Yankees versus those from fans of the Red Sox. I think prayers are for us.*

I empathize with my friend's view. It strikes me as honest, willing to cast the conversation about prayer more in mystery than manipulation. Prayers are for us. They engage our spirits in a conscious inner acknowledgment that our lives bear both the mark and need of God's moving among and working through us. Prayers are for us. That's also an interesting angle from which to view Jesus' prayer in the presence of those gathered at Lazarus's tomb: *Father, I thank you for having heard me. I knew that you always hear me, but I have said this for the sake of the crowd standing here.* Jesus prays in recognition and affirmation of God's hearing. But the thrust of his words reveals that the prayer is not for Jesus' sake and not even God's sake, but for the sake of those gathered. Jesus prays for the sake of others, so that they may hear that God hears.

Believing that God hears can be an extraordinary leap of faith. Such a leap may not seem significant in ordinary and routine times, when in the peace and plenty of our lives we pray with absolute certainty that God hears. But that leap of faith may be required when we lift prayers in times of crisis: at the hospital bed of a loved one struggling for life; in a counselor's office when a marriage continues to spin out of control; or, as is the case for Jesus, at the grave of a loved one. Sometimes when we pray, our words or thoughts may disappear into what seems a deafening silence, swallowed up by the enormity of what we face. The next time you experience such a silence, listen to Jesus' prayer in a new way: *I knew that you always hear me, but I have said this for the sake of* _____, and fill in the blank with your name. Christ prays before the tomb of Lazarus for the sake of anyone whose life poises at the edge, where God's hearing of prayer comes as no easy assumption but a part of faith's venture of trust.

God hears prayers. How exactly remains a mystery. But if John's text can be trusted, God hears. God hears the prayers we speak aloud. God hears the prayers we lift in silence. God even hears when words for prayer escape us, through the Spirit who "intercedes with sighs too deep for words" (Rom. 8:26). We may pray in difficult situations, when we bring no answers but only questions, with the assurance that we do not speak into the void. We speak to One who hears even a child with two hundred broken bones and parents with two broken hearts; a hearing, we pray, that will someday and someplace issue in that child's knowing the joy of wind rushing through hair as he runs without fear and leaps without pain. So let us pray, for God does hear.

You hear me, O God. You know my voice. You see my heart. Help me to pray, not so much to convince you of who I am and what I need but to help me understand who I am and what I need. And in my understanding, help me to be caring and concerned for others and for this world so loved by you. Amen.

Spiritual Exercise

As you pray, listen to the words and thoughts you bring to God. Imagine how God might hear their focus, emotion, and "cast of characters." In your journal, write what these prayers reveal of you. Ask yourself, How do my prayers truly reflect the breadth of my life and concerns? Journal ideas that might help you integrate your life and concerns into your prayers. Then pray with an awareness and appreciation that God hears you.

Day 7

TRANSFIGURATION

And while [Jesus] was praying, the appearance of his face changed
and his clothes became dazzling white. . . .
"This is my Son, my Chosen; listen to him!"
—Luke 9:29, 35

RANSFIGURATION. JESUS' CLOTHES became dazzling white. His face shone—in Matthew's words, "like the sun." Moses and Elijah appeared. A voice spoke from a cloud. Something happened on that mountain. But what . . . and why?

The Greek word used by the Gospels of Mark and Matthew to describe this event is *metamorphoo*, from which we get our word *metamorphose*. The language and details of the story suggest that what happens to Jesus on the mountain involves inward as well as outward change. Luke and the other Gospel writers leave the *process* of Transfiguration a mystery, much as they leave what happens between midnight of Holy Saturday and dawn of Easter Sunday without description. *Transfiguration*, like Resurrection, remains a concept of faith rather than a category of science.

Prayer figured into the equation of life changed, "transfigured," though exactly how remains part of the mystery. We do not know the words Jesus offers in prayer, only that they come eight days after the first announcement of suffering and death and rising. They come eight days after the first invitation to bear a cross, to journey in the revelation that holding on to life is the last way to save it. In other words, the prayer comes eight days after all bets are off about things continuing as they always have. New ways and fresh choices loom ahead. To be in prayer in such a time about such concerns can be transfiguring.

Prayer and transformation belong together. When we enter into God's presence and open our lives to the possibilities of God, things change. We change—not magically but spiritually. The connection between the change manifested on the Mount of Transfiguration and the change God would bring to our lives is not sleight of hand, or smoke and mirrors, or illusions that fool the eye. Change crafted by God intends to turn life and heart around.

Jesus is not the only one who sets foot on the mountain. As Jesus does elsewhere, he takes others with him to pray. They see the change in the Teacher. Glowing face and dazzling clothes make an impression, a far greater impression than words of cross-bearing and discipleship spoken eight days earlier. Transfiguration changes Jesus' appearance. But the real question remains whether the Transfiguration will change the hearts of disciples not yet ready to exchange their hopes of a conquering hero for the truth of a suffering messiah. Such change cannot be perceived on the surface of things, yet it penetrates the heart and spills out into our living and our following.

This prayer that Jesus offers on the roadside, on the Mount of Transfiguration, provides neither the disciples nor us with any incantations we might repeat to put a glow on our cheeks or to dazzle others with our appearance. In the end, the story provides its own interpretive clue as to the why of Transfiguration prayer. *This is my Son, my Chosen; listen to him!*

Listen. Transfiguration, spiritual transformation, begins in that simple admonishment. Listen. Listen to the One who prefaces affirmations of rising with warnings of suffering. Listen to the One who challenges us to loosen our grasp on life at all costs in order to have life in its fullness. Listen.

The last of Jesus' roadside prayers considered here issues in this plea, this discipline, to listen. You and I would do well to keep it in mind and heart. Prayer can devolve into an awful chore if we feel it is up to us to bring everything in need of change before God: lives in need of fixing, relationships in need of mending, a world in need of peace-ing together. If such habits tilt your prayers too much toward advising God as to how this change must happen (how God must be God), then remember a mount, a glowing face, and dazzling clothes. Once your attention is captured, listen. Listen in prayer. Listen *as* prayer.

Transform me, O God, not for appearance's sake but for goodness' sake. Amen.

Spiritual Exercise

When have you experienced change in the midst or as a result of prayer? What did that change consist of? How did you maintain the change over time? Write your reflections on this experience in your journal. As you do, think about your practice of prayer and how it incorporates listening. Note some ways in which you could practice prayer as an act of listening as well as speaking or thinking; for example, reading a verse of scripture or listening to a piece of music, with no agenda save being in God's presence. Incorporate one of those ways into your prayers this day and through this week, to practice the discipline of prayerful listening.

WEEK THREE

On the Mountainside

Day 1

ALL THINGS NECESSARY

MATTHEW 6:9-13

*Y*OU ARE STRANDED *on a desert island. A box washes ashore. In it are seven items. Much to your amazement, they are the very seven things you need most to live. What would those seven items be? What would make them necessary?*

I engaged in an exercise similar to this one at the beginning of a curriculum writers' and editors' conference. Some of us had never met the other folks there, and this activity became a helpful way to introduce ourselves on a slightly deeper level than simply "Tell us your name, where you're from, and what's your favorite color." It makes for a good icebreaker at youth groups or topic of conversation at a dinner party. But consider this spinoff of the exercise.

You walk into the chapel of a long abandoned monastery. You see a crumpled note on the altar. It reads, "Those who pray here may only do so for all things necessary for life, and the prayer must be seventy-five words or less." You kneel at the altar. What few words will you pray to keep faith with this tradition? Seeing a candle on the altar, you strike a match and light the wick. The flame illuminates a wooden panel against the wall behind the altar, with letters covered in dust. You wipe the dust with your jacket sleeve and stand back to read the words: "Our Father. . . ."

The answer to question 118 in the Heidelberg Catechism about what God commands us to ask in prayer goes as follows: "All things necessary for soul and body, which Christ our Lord has comprised in the prayer taught us by Himself." Week in and week out, sometimes day in and day out, persons and communities of faith offer the words of the Lord's Prayer, the Our Father, or whatever title we lend to Jesus' example of prayer for all things necessary.

Two accounts of the Lord's Prayer come to us, one in Luke and one in Matthew. Luke's account is a slight abbreviation of Matthew's. Luke sets the prayer in a private time of instruction in response to a disciple's question about how to pray. Matthew places the prayer amidst crowds gathered for the Sermon on the Mount. As Moses brought the Law from Mount Sinai to Israel as directions for keeping the covenant, so Jesus offers a mountainside "sermon" that reveals what living in this new covenant requires. At the heart of that sermon, both structurally and theologically, stands Jesus' example of prayer (*The New Interpreter's Bible*, vol. 8 [Nashville, Tenn.: Abingdon Press, 1995], 202). This prayer and our praying in the example of Jesus thus stands at the core of the covenant God enters with us. This week's readings will follow the text of the prayer as recorded in Matthew.

The immediate context for Jesus' example of prayer in Matthew arises out of two critiques of prayer. "Do not be like the hypocrites," Matthew 6:5 begins. Jesus aims his warning at those who make public shows out of prayer "so that they may be seen by others." When prayer becomes a civic showcase or media production to make points, whether religious, political, or otherwise, these words of Jesus caution us to recall prayer's rooting in a heartfelt conversation with God. Spiritual depth is not revealed in prayer as public relations. The beginning of Jesus' example of prayer invokes the only audience of concern: Our Father.

The second critique runs a slightly different course: "Do not heap up empty phrases as the Gentiles . . . think[ing] that they will be heard because of their many words" (6:7). Some religious traditions fashion prayer wheels to spin in the wind, based on the belief that each rotation offers the prayer again. More rotations equal more prayers. An equivalent tradition in Christianity comes in the long-worded (if not long-winded) prayer. More words equal better prayers—or pray-ers. In the face of these ageless inclinations, Jesus counsels another way. *Pray then in this way* (6:9) is not a decree to memorize the Lord's Prayer so we can have familiar words with which to close worship or end the pastoral prayer. *Pray then in this way* invites us to form our prayer life in simplicity and brevity, cutting to the core of what is truly necessary for soul, body, and life.

The prayer itself hinges on a marvelous balance between what we offer to God and what we seek from God. Your name, your kingdom, your will—we enter into the prayer by confessing to God our respect and honor and hope. Prayer begins in acknowledgment of God's presence. Our spiritual formation in the light of this prayer resides in the affirmation that our first steps, our first words, always belong to and trace from God. What we seek in life begins by confessing what God seeks for life. Thus we pray for necessities.

The grace of God bids us to bring our most pressing needs into the conversation that is prayer: our bread, our debts, our deliverance. Jesus' example of prayer and prayerful living does not leave us to fend for ourselves in a world where food, forgiveness, and freedom do not always come easily.

Throughout the prayer, praise and confession are always expressed in the first-person plural: our, we, us. Jesus' example of prayer assumes community. Even when we offer these words in solitude, we do so as part of God's called community and with the Christ who teaches us so to pray. Jesus' instruction to *pray then in this way* imprints our prayers with the mark of belonging, the mark of connection, the mark of *koinonia* ("common life"). Spiritual formation is not a task undertaken in isolation, by lone individuals struggling to achieve independence before God. Spiritual formation in the light of Jesus' prayer bids us into community in our involvements, in our prayers, in "all things necessary for soul and body." For God has so formed us to live, and Christ has so taught us to pray.

God of light, teach me again to pray. In Christ's example, to your glory. For others' sake. Teach me again to pray. Amen.

Spiritual Exercise

What are some of your early associations or memories of the Lord's Prayer? Whose voices do you recall offering it with you or teaching it to you? In your journal, reflect on times when this prayer has been especially meaningful in your life and in the life of congregations of which you have been a part. Note the circumstances that created those special meanings. Consider what you learned about prayer in those experiences. Say the Lord's Prayer aloud. Pray it in sections, leaving silence between its petitions to allow you opportunity to linger over its words and their meanings. At its end, offer a prayer of thanks for its gift. Close by praying aloud the prayer printed above ("Teach me . . . ").

Day 2

HOLY THE NAME

"Our Father in heaven, hallowed be your name."
—Matthew 6:9

AMES. IN OUR EARLIEST days, we begin to recognize a sound repeated time and again by parents or guardians. Of all the sounds our ears take in, we gradually come to understand that a particular sound means "me." We learn it as a sound voiced to gain attention, to speak love, to whisper comfort. It is *our* name. We come to learn other sounds, other names upon which we can call with a question, for help, in joy, out of fear. The bestowing of our name gives us identity. The bestowing of another's name gives us access. Jesus' example of prayer begins with the gift of a name and with a task attached to that name.

Our Father in heaven. In these four words Jesus teaches us the name of the One we address in prayer: the One who is source of life, figure of strength, and a host of other images drawn from the best human experience of "fathering." Addressing God as Father is no more a statement of gender than referring to Christ as the Solid Rock is an expression of Jesus' mineral content. The imagery of God as Father intends to affirm a childlike relationship of trust. Through Christ we are graced to address God by this very personal name.

Because the human experience of fathering varies widely, prayer to God as Father will come easier for some and with more difficulty for others. When you offer the opening words of this prayer, does the title flow easily and naturally? Does it stumble on painful remembrances or inhibiting societal structures? If the latter, may you find a way to reclaim the name or find a new one that conveys the loving and nurturing image it intends.

Take note of the pronoun that opens the prayer, not "my" but "our." We pray according to Jesus' example when we pray to One who is not a private possession or a church's peculiar truth or even a nation's exclusive guardian, but to one who is *our* Father. Think of that for a moment. Whenever we offer this prayer, we make a statement about everyone in its hearing. Jesus does not teach us: "Say, 'Our Father,' unless there are Presbyterians, Roman Catholics, Jews, or Muslims in the room." We pray to the One who is our Father, no matter who is present. When we pray as Jesus instructs us we consider not only who God is but who we are to one another. No matter whose face we see, we look into the eyes of another child of God. No exceptions. Period. How can we be earnest in this prayer's recitation yet equally diligent in prejudice or hatred or exclusion? We need to be more careful in our prayers. God might hold us accountable for words like *Our Father*.

Hallowed be your name. For some, keeping God's name holy entails seeing to it that others do not think that God's last name is damn. Without a doubt, the casual use of expletives or the peppering of everyday conversation with a host of "Jesus Christs!" cheapens the holiness of God's name.

Merely to avoid certain expressions, however, does not fulfill the charge to keep God's name holy. Though we pray to God for the hallowing of God's name, the task of doing so is *ours*, not God's. Our whole lives witness to the holiness of God within us. Do others see in our conduct and conversations reason to hold God's name holy? Or do they sense in us a disconnect between the hymns we sing or creeds we recite on

Sundays and the respect we give others and God in the ethics that guide our everyday decisions? The hallowing of God's name may begin in the prayer closet, but it takes shape in our living in the world.

Our Father in heaven, hallowed be your name. Christ graces us with the privilege to call upon God in prayer by name. So graced, may we keep holy the name of God in the whole of our lives.

Loving Mother and Father of all creation, of all your children: You breathe life into my name. May my breath keep holy your name in word and in deed, in prayer and in service. In Jesus Christ. Amen.

Spiritual Exercise

Pray the Lord's Prayer, placing "Our Father" (or the name that speaks that depth of relationship for you) before every petition (*"Our Father, your kingdom come; our Father, your will be done..."*). Reflect on the influence of this name's repetition on the prayer's sound, meaning, and intimacy. In your journal, reflect on what "hallowing the name of God" means for you personally. Identify three ways your prayers and actions can hallow God's name. Use those three ways in your devotional life and daily life beginning today (or tomorrow, if you do this reading at night).

Day 3

TENACITY

"Your kingdom come. Your will be done, on earth as it is in heaven."
—Matthew 6:10

SEVERAL MONTHS into my first pastorate, I visited the home of Phil and Winnie LaSota. During the first hour or so, Winnie and I did most of the talking while Phil remained relatively quiet in his chair. At some point, however, whether because he decided he could trust me or because of his love of telling stories, Phil began to talk about his life.

For the next two hours, and in subsequent visits, Phil treated me to an excursion into living history. First came the young Phil, journeying west at the turn of the nineteenth century to Spokane, cooking for an upstart restaurant and hotel entrepreneur named Louis Davenport. Then there was Phil the homesteader, building a log home by the headwaters of the Little Pend Oreille River. There was Phil the forest service cook, who with his crew was trapped by the great St. Joe fire in northern Idaho that burned the land between the St. Joe River and Kellogg and Wallace. They survived only by digging into the banks of a small creek and soaking their blankets to cover their backs, then listening to the fire rage over them. Then came Phil the community leader, who successfully led the fight to prevent the internment of the Kubota family during the Second World War.

Of all my memories of Phil, what struck me most was his tenacious hope. Phil held mineral rights to a parcel of land north of Metaline Falls. Convinced it held a workable deposit of lead and silver, he spent his early retirement years regularly and faithfully working the claim. When his legs gave out, Phil transferred the rights to his nephew, believing that someday the claim would pay off. During my time there, Phil slowly but surely lost ground. First came confinement to his home, then to his chair, then to his bed. His mobility steadily deserted him, but not his hope. Flat on his back, he still talked of the claim and his certainty of its coming through. Unable to walk, he still looked forward. When we buried Phil, we celebrated not only a colorful past but an unyielding hope. He would not let it go.

For nearly two thousand years, the church has prayed these petitions: *Your kingdom come. Your will be done.* During our whole lifetimes in church, we plead for the in-breaking of God's sovereign realm and the doing of God's will. Some, perhaps many, might say we are no closer to those becoming realities in our lifetime than was Phil's hope of his claim coming through for him. In a society in which instant gratification is a rampant disease, when we grow impatient with the seconds it takes for computers to load screens and start programs, prayers and hopes that linger beyond the horizons of lifetimes, not to mention millennia, are not easily offered and held.

Yet square in the middle of Jesus' example of prayer are these two petitions. They present us with a choice. We can offer them by rote, quickly reciting the words so that we don't have to think about the passage of centuries between Jesus' first utterance of them and our shallow recitation. Or we can allow them to permeate our prayers and service with an unyielding tenacity and hope.

These words form us in the truth that our lives and prayers will necessarily introduce a certain spirit of discontent into our earthly sojourn. Praying for God's realm reaffirms the unsatisfied longing that life holds more than is readily available at the moment. Praying for the doing of God's will turns the prayer from intercession into offering. The hope of the realization of

God's will is not mere wishful thinking or wistful longing about what is right or just or merciful. It is not even about what God will do apart from our prayers. *Your will be done* boomerangs into our acknowledgment of God's will for and the offering of ourselves in God's service: "Here I am."

Your kingdom come. Your will be done. The searching nature of these petitions echoes strongly in a text from Hebrews:

> *For people who speak in this way make it clear that they are seeking a homeland. If they had been thinking of the land that they had left behind, they would have had opportunity to return. But as it is, they desire a better country, that is, a heavenly one.* (11:14-16)

To be a people who pray for God's kingdom forms us into a people of hope, unwilling to settle for lesser imitations packaged in the status quo or world-weary pessimisms. To be a people who pray for the doing of God's will draws us into the prayer's very fulfillment. May we pray with such tenacity in hope as Phil LaSota lived and as Jesus seeks from those who commit prayer and life to nothing less than God's own realm and will.

Your realm, O God, and your will: may I not cease in their praying; may I not despair in their living; may I not yield in their hope. In Jesus Christ. Amen.

Spiritual Exercise

Reflect on an aspect of your life that troubles you. Prayerfully consider and write in your journal what the realization of God's realm in that area of your life might mean and what the doing of God's will might look like. Commit yourself to daily prayer and personal action that seek God's realm and will.

Consider extending this exercise to an area of your church, your community, the world. If you do this, consider working with one or two persons. Identify together an area of concern you share about your church, your community, or the wider world. Prayerfully reflect on how God's coming realm might lead you to witness and service.

Day 4

BREAD FOR THE DAY

"Give us this day our daily bread."
—Matthew 6:11

BREAD. HOW COMMON and ordinary bread is. We rarely think of eating bread alone anymore, unless it's still warm from the oven. We tend now to think of bread smeared with jelly to flavor it or covered with slices of lunch meat to add substance or spread with butter, which, if turned down, makes people wonder why on earth anyone would want to eat plain, dry bread. Bread has become a mere accessory to meals today.

It has not always been so. In Hebrew, the word for ordinary bread and the word for food are one and the same. Perhaps the most famous story of bread in the Hebrew Bible comes in the gift of manna in the wilderness. "Behold, I will rain bread from heaven for you; and the people shall go out and gather a day's portion every day" (Exod. 16:4, RSV). God provided so that "the Israelites ate manna forty years" (Exod. 16:35). Forty years on bread. A prisoner's diet is God's gift of providence to those newly freed.

Curiously the manna given each day in the wilderness satisfied the need for food, regardless of how much or how little was required: "Those who gathered much had nothing over, and those who gathered little had no shortage" (Exod. 16:18). The daily gift of manna was sufficient to feed everyone who hungered, sufficient for that day's journey. In addition, this bread could not be stored away for either profit or gluttony: "Some left part of it until the morning, and it bred worms and became foul" (Exod. 16:20, RSV). The manna was given by God for that one day. No more, no less. The only exception came on the day before sabbath, when a sufficient supply was provided for that day and the sabbath, so that sabbath could be kept. Manna was, literally, *daily* bread.

Give us this day our daily bread. Manna. Daily bread. The prayer Jesus teaches us to pray is not one that conjures up overladen tables and multiple refrigerators stocked to overflowing. We pray for daily bread, sufficient for our day's need, sufficient for our sojourn in the wilderness. What do you require for life and living? Providence invites you to pray.

Give us this day our daily bread. The prayer not only offers a personal intercession, but it invites a humbling assessment of the community we keep with others. An enormous divergence exists between what most of us presume to be daily bread and those for whom daily bread falls somewhere between faint hope and bitter struggle. To pray Jesus' words bids us exhibit Jesus' compassion. To be spiritually formed by this petition bids our recognition of and participation in the community that its words imply. *Our* daily bread seats us at a table wide enough to encompass all those whom *our* God calls children. If our plates stack full to overflowing while that of the person across from us sits empty and bare, how can we pray this prayer and close our eyes to the discrepancy? How can we offer these words to God and not consider that the bounty enjoyed by some is intended for the nourishment of all?

Give us this day our daily bread. The heart of this petition confesses a radical dependence upon God for the ordinary necessities of life. The challenge of this prayer is in reclaiming a renewed vision of what embodies necessity and in demonstrating generosity with all that goes beyond any day's need.

That reclamation forms a genuine spiritual discipline, for it returns us to a deeper sense of dependence on God. Abundance does not bless us, define us, or provide "our daily bread." For true sustenance we pray to and trust in God. May we exercise generosity toward others modeled on the grace of God's providence.

I pray for bread sufficient for this day, O God. May I break my bread with others so that your grace might feed us both. In Jesus Christ. Amen.

Spiritual Exercise

In your journal, inventory what you consider bare necessities for your life: material, emotional, spiritual. Give thanks for the ways in which you experience God providing for these needs. Identify individuals or groups you see who struggle to find such necessities met in these same areas of life: material, emotional, or spiritual (one person or group for each area). Commit yourself to daily prayer for these persons and to one specific act that might be of help to each. Pray that they might find the daily bread they need. If you find yourself in such need of daily bread, pray this petition of the prayer, naming your need aloud. Seek help from others. Trust in God's providence.

Day 5

FORGIVE

"Forgive us our debts, as we also have forgiven our debtors."
—Matthew 6:12

*D*RIVING HOME ONE afternoon, I listened to a radio
station broadcasting from Seattle. One of its news-
casts carried the story of the trial of a young man
charged with vehicular manslaughter. He had hit a three-year-
old girl with his car, panicked, and sped off. The report included a portion of the testimony of the dead child's mother.
Anger rose in her voice as she looked squarely at the defendant
and addressed her comments at him, though, the reporter
noted, he would not or could not bring himself to look at her.
She said what angered her most was his leaving the scene and
his absence from the hospital as the child's family waited to
hear the eventual tragic news. The mother said she wished the
defendant had been there so she could have told him that
sometimes things happen so fast we cannot do anything about
them. But he wasn't there. And she was angry at that man.
Angry, to be sure, at her daughter's death and his cowardly
flight, but angry also that he had robbed her of the opportunity to forgive him at a time when that word might have been
healing to both of them.

Forgive. A very simple word for a very powerful gift. Jesus'
prayer makes the simplicity of forgiveness even more stark,
even more powerful. *Forgive us . . . as we also have forgiven.* Consider the implication of this plea: "God, be just as gracious and

forgiving toward me as you see me being toward others." Now that is not an easy prayer to raise, except perhaps for a person with a terminal case of pride who presumes the petition can be offered glibly without concern for consequences.

Forgive us . . . as we also have forgiven. Does Jesus really mean that? We all want God to be gracious and forgiving toward us. But do we want God to be as forgiving toward us as we are toward others? That is how and what Jesus teaches us to pray in this petition: to be forgiven by God as we are forgiving toward those who wrong us. Anybody uncomfortable yet?

Other folks had trouble with the petition about forgiveness right from the beginning. Why else would this be the only verse of the prayer to generate its own commentary by Jesus?

> *"For if you forgive others their trespasses, your heavenly Father will also forgive you; but if you do not forgive others, neither will your Father forgive your trespasses."* (vv. 14-15)

Later on in Matthew's Gospel, Peter asks Jesus about the upper limits of such forgiveness. "Lord, how often shall my brother sin against me, and I forgive him? As many as seven times?" (Matt. 18:21). Among the rabbis of that day, seven represented the upper limit placed on the obligation of forgiveness, with many arguing for less. In our day, conventional wisdom tends to settle for an even shorter obligation. "Fool me once, shame on you; fool me twice, shame on me." Jesus, however, has other ideas. "Not seven times, but, I tell you, seventy-seven times" (Matt. 18:22). Jesus' point is not mathematical but theological—as often as needed, forgive.

Forgive us . . . as we also have forgiven. Before we hear in Matthew a story or a parable or any other information about forgiveness, Jesus teaches us to pray for forgiveness and a forgiving spirit. Knowledge and information about forgiveness, though helpful, do not engage one in its practice. Prayer does. Prayer that hopes to enter the presence of God recognizes that Christ's example of forgiveness opens the way for us to approach God. Such prayer brings us into the presence of the One who receives us in grace and sends us forth to offer graciousness toward others. We do not forgive in order to be forgiven. That would be mere works-righteousness. No, we forgive because we have been forgiven, grateful for what we have received and full of hope for what our forgiving may make possible.

Forgive us . . . as we also have forgiven. To travel the prayer paths of Jesus means to extend the grace of Jesus. So forgiven, so forgive.

Blur the line, O God, between my being forgiven and my being forgiving. Let me not fuss about where one ends and the other begins, for both end and begin in you. Amen.

Spiritual Exercise

Draw a line that divides a page in your journal in two. On one side, write what (whom) you currently find it hard to forgive. Be specific. On the other side of the line, write down what or from whom you currently find it hard to accept forgiveness. Pray for situations in which your forgiveness and your forgiving are tested. Reflect on connections between the two sides of your journal page. Pray today's petition in the first-person singular ("Forgive me my sins, as I also have forgiven those who have sinned against me"). Seek God's help in allowing both elements of the prayer to root you more deeply in a life formed by forgiveness.

Day 6

TRIAL AND DELIVERANCE

"Do not bring us to the time of trial, but rescue us from the evil one."
—Matthew 6:13

*T*HEY SAY CONFESSION is good for the soul, so here goes: My favorite hobby relies on the art of temptation. I tie flies and cast them upon waters in hopes of enticing a trout into a strike. Some of the patterns I tie and cast sink to fish holding in deep lies or swift currents. Others skim the surface film of a lake or ride the riffle of a stream. Some represent exact imitations of a particular insect hatching at a specific time. Others just look buggy. Some are so tiny as to be dwarfed by mosquitoes, others large enough to put a fair-sized bruise on the back of my head if I do not cast carefully. But they all serve one purpose: to tempt a fish.

Does this correspond to your idea about how temptation comes? Is God the skilled fisher who crafts each lure according to your weakness, presenting it in such a way to see if you will meet the test? *Let's see, John has a tendency to gossip. So let's drift a #12 Rumor by him and see if he bites or keeps it to himself. . . .*

Surely God wouldn't test us in such ways! But why then would Jesus bother to ask in this prayer about life's necessities that we not be brought to trial or, in more familiar words: "Lead us not into temptation" (KJV)? Perhaps we deal with the tension caused by the fear of trial by making distinctions between tempting and testing.

Temptation implies a direct appeal to evil. Our society, if not at times the church, tends to portray temptation in its "flashier" or more exciting enticements of sex, drugs, or power. Yet where most folks live, temptation comes more subtly. We are far more likely to succumb to temptation in the quiet ways of our ordinary lives, settling for lower standards of ethics or character than we are capable of. Daily temptations lure us without need of God's casting the line.

But rescue us from the evil one. Jesus' example of prayer creates the image and hope of God as One who rescues us from evil's power if not presence. Evil finds ready incarnation in extraordinary events of gross inhumanity: at Tiananmen Square or Auschwitz, in a massacre at Wounded Knee or the rubble of the World Trade Center. When evil reaches such horrifying proportions, few are tempted to remain its allies and advocates.

But there is another evil from which God would deliver us. It takes a more pernicious shape, one that sometimes passes for respectability or popularity or religiosity. Such evil reduces us to silence when another goes ridiculed or abused, lest our defense of that person place us or those we love at risk. Such evil may use the name of God to justify all manner of prejudice, greed, and personal irresponsibility. *Deliver us from evil.*

You and I do not pray Jesus' prayer in the fullness of God's reign within this world, when this petition no longer will have any meaning. We know the places in our own lives where we are sorely tested, where faith and goodness compete with powerful and persuasive adversaries for our allegiance. We also know where evil resides, sometimes too close to home, sometimes too attractive and appealing for our own good. Traveling the prayer paths of Jesus does not provide us with an escape but with a means to live and choose faithfully in the midst of captivating alternatives. *Do not bring us to the time of trial, but rescue us from the evil one.* When testing comes and evil draws near, Jesus' prayer offers us the promise and hope of God, whose desire is not to tempt our weaknesses but to redeem our lives.

*Strong and tender Redeemer, if I should withdraw from you when test-
ing comes or evil looms, draw me back to you. Be present with me in
those times to restore my courage, to strengthen my will, to help me
trust your grace. Amen.*

Spiritual Exercise

Set aside at least ten minutes to be alone. Say today's petition
from Jesus' prayer aloud. Observe a time of silence. What one
or two words from the prayer echo in your mind or spirit? Repeat aloud the prayer petition. Pause for silence. What situations in your life or in your community come to your mind?
Continue with this pattern of offering the petition and allowing a subsequent time of silent reflection. Journal your
thoughts and impressions of this prayer experience. Find a way
to incorporate these situations into your prayers this day.

Day 7

PUNCTUATION MARKS

"For the kingdom and the power and the glory
are yours forever. Amen."
—Matthew 6:13

*W*HEN I BEGAN to prepare manuscripts that would pass before the scrutiny of editors, I had to re-learn the art of punctuation. Writing sermons, the text of which no one usually sees except myself, provides the luxury of being somewhat lazy about rules my English teachers spent years getting through to me. In preaching, I could depend upon my voice to punctuate the feeling of a sentence: to have it flow to a definitive break (.), or construct a query (?), or quietly trail off to encourage reflection (. . .), or build to a shout (!).

Of all the marks of punctuation, exclamation points present the greatest challenge to me. Without them, words may communicate no points of emphasis, no stirrings of heart and will into action. But English teachers of old, as well as present writing mentors, encourage a sparse use of them. Abundant exclamation points lose their ability to surprise or excite or jolt us. They should be timed and spaced to keep their power intact.

Our lives remind us of moving with such a rhythm. Ordinarily we pass through life with occasional exclamation points marking the landscape: the birth of a child, a promotion at work, a long-awaited reunion, an unusually beautiful sunset, an extraordinary moment of experiencing God's grace anew.

Such times do not usually come to us hourly or daily, not even weekly or monthly. Their uniqueness and power derive from the routine of our lives. The best of them create a vista to recall in the mind's eye, an encouragement to persevere. All of them exclaim life's gift.

For the kingdom and the power and the glory are yours forever. Amen. In reading the text for this day, you might have found this sentence missing from your translation. Most Bibles include it only as a footnote. How could translators leave out a passage we all know by heart? In fact, the oldest manuscripts of Matthew, not yet discovered when the King James Bible (whose Matthew 6:13 *does* include the line) appeared, do not contain this doxology. Biblical scholars note its close parallel to 1 Chronicles 29:11 and suggest that the footnote became a traditional response of the community to the prayer of Jesus offered in early worship. Which is to say, these words became the prayer's exclamation point!

And why not? This prayer offers extraordinary gifts of access and vocation and intercession to those who pray in the example and spirit of Jesus. We are called to hallow God's name, serve God's sovereign realm, and enact God's will; graced to intercede for daily bread, receive and offer forgiveness, and be led from trial and evil. Can somebody give me an amen?

For the kingdom and the power and the glory are yours. Since the earliest days of the church, the community of faith has ended the prayer of Jesus with an exclamation point about God's authority, ability, and presence.

The *kingdom:* All of our allegiances stand under the scrutiny and judgment of our confession. The exclamation point of God's authority punctuates our loyalties.

The *power:* The word in Greek is *dunamis*, the root of "dynamite." Power refers to sheer, raw ability. No powers on this earth rival the power of God for good, for compassion, for grace. Once we declare where power resides, we confirm to whom the future belongs.

The *glory:* The glory of God in the Hebrew Bible came revealed in the cloud that led Israel through the wilderness. Glory affirms, as does this prayer, God's saving presence on a journey that leads to life.

Pray the Lord's Prayer. Punctuate it with these closing words of exclamation. In prayer, you join a line whose beginning and end stretch far beyond your sight and experience, yet never out of sight or embrace of God. In prayer, you add your voice to the chorus who prays and sings in every tongue imaginable, yet who speaks as one. *For the kingdom and the power and the glory are yours forever.*

And let the people say, *Amen and amen!*

When I feel low, when I question what difference faith makes, teach me again, Lord Jesus, the art of your exclamation points of grace, hope, and glory. Amen.

Spiritual Exercise

What excites you about faith, about living in God's presence? Write your thoughts in your journal. As you record them, offer thanks for each one of these "exclamation points." Pray the Lord's Prayer aloud in this manner: After each phrase or petition, offer the prayer's "exclamation point" (Our Father in heaven, hallowed be your name, *the kingdom and the power and the glory are yours forever,* your kingdom come, for the kingdom . . .). Offer aloud as a prayer the thoughts you wrote in the journal, and conclude them with "for the kingdom . . . "

WEEK FOUR

In the Upper Room

Day 1

THE PEOPLE WHO PRAY FOR US

JOHN 17:1-26

*W*HOSE VOICE OFFERING your name in prayer would most comfort and strengthen you? At the age of ten I underwent an appendectomy at De-Paul Hospital in St. Louis. Two distinct memories stay with me from that experience. First, I suffered a serious crush on my nurse. *Suffer* is the proper word to describe the unrequited love of a preadolescent, though I find now that I can no longer remember the name of her around whom my world revolved for my five or so days at DePaul. Second, a priest prayed for me. It was evening, or at least the room seemed darkened. My Protestant upbringing had not prepared me for the sight of one so ornately vested with that strange pointed hat I came to know later as a miter. I seem to recall that as he stood at the foot of the bed, I felt a mix of wonder and fear. I did not know him, and he did not look like people I did know. But he prayed for me. I do not recall what he prayed. It might have been in Latin, for all I can remember. But he prayed. For me. He took time to bring my name and need before God. That I knew. That I still know. That I carry with me in ministry.

Since then I have heard my name and need spoken in prayer by others in times of celebration, in times of grieving, in times of passage. The act of being prayed for by another is an extraordinary gift. Even if the one who prays does not know wholly what may confront, threaten, or uplift you in that moment, he or she has taken the time and care to bring your name and life before the One who is Author and Hope of all life. As I reflect on those moments of hearing and feeling myself the beneficiary of prayer, a sense of something akin to gratitude—only much deeper—comes to mind and heart.

Admittedly, we would prefer that some persons voice our name in prayer rather than others. Occasionally individuals may publicly lift our name in prayer in ways we may feel to be paternalistic if not demeaning. In such instances prayer can become a bludgeon. "Please help Brother Bill with his inability to be compassionate. And forgive, O Lord, Sister Martha for her mistakes in ministry at our church."

But even in the wrongheadedness (or hard-heartedness) of some prayers, any effort made to lift an individual before God offers a glimmer of hope and care. For though we may have the assessment of an individual, her situation, or her needs all wrong, God knows what is right and best and good. God can work through the misconceptions that would otherwise cloud understanding of the one for whom we pray. Whatever our motives, God will hear and know and seek what is good.

So, who prays for you? Who lifts up to God your life, your journey, your hopes, your fears? Imagine for a moment the person whom you most trust and respect. Imagine that individual now lifting to God your needs and joys, praying for God's presence with you. You know that person's voice. You have heard that voice speak words of truth, words of insight, perhaps words of love. Consider now the sound of that voice as it bears you up to God in prayer.

"I ask not only on behalf of these, but also on behalf of those who will believe in me through their word" (John 17:20). Jesus prays for you.

Scholars sometimes label this chapter in John's Gospel Jesus' "high priestly prayer." The designation draws on the image of

Jesus interceding with God on behalf of the community, as did the high priest of Israel. However, in contrast to the high priest who prepared sacrificial offerings, Jesus himself will become the sacrificial offering in John's narrative.

Normally we consider prayer as the words we bring to God, even to Jesus. But in John's Gospel we overhear Jesus praying not just for strangers who lived two millennia past, but for persons who live today—for you and me. We do not have to imagine the sound of Jesus forming our name in prayer, for in the verses encountered in this week's readings, we will overhear Jesus' prayers for us. The One whose voice stilled waves and calmed troubled spirits, spoke truth to power and love to outcasts, that One prays for us by name intercedes for the need we bear most deeply: "so that the love with which you have loved me may be in them, . . . and I in them" (John 17:26).

The people who pray for us are important companions on life's journey. Some pray for us out of familial love. Saint Augustine considered his mother's prayers among the chief influences that led to his faith conversion. Parent, spouse, and child seek the best for one another; prayer affords opportunity to lift families up to God's good purposes. Others pray for us out of friendship or the sense of belonging nurtured in Christian community. Worship provides regular moments of lifting in prayer to God persons not only from the congregation but from the wider community. When we hear our names spoken in prayer by those voices we most love, trust, and respect, we cannot help but feel nourished, embraced, and empowered.

What does it mean for us to know that the One in whose name we gather speaks your name, your life, in prayer? What does it mean for you to be an individual, to be part of a community, for whom Jesus prays?

Throughout this week, listen as Jesus prays for us. For you.

I thank you, O God, for all those who bring my name and person and need to you in prayer. I thank you, Lord Jesus, for your prayers for me. As you pray, may I live. Amen.

Spiritual Exercise

Make two lists in your journal. The first is a list of all the persons you prayed for in the last week, and why. The second is a list of the persons you would like to pray for you. Reflect on why you would like them to pray for you. Tonight, or whenever you keep a regular time of prayer, pray for the persons on the first list, then for those on the second list. Pray for the needs you see them bearing and for the joys you understand they experience. Pray that you will be remembered in someone's prayers tonight, and add a new person not on either list to your prayers. Close with a prayer of thanks for Jesus' prayer for you.

Day 2

"Do You Know What Time It Is?"

Jesus . . . looked up to heaven and said, "Father, the hour has come."
—John 17:1

WARM SUMMER MORNINGS. The smell of sawdust and oil paints. Paper cups of ice cream with wooden spoons in white wrappers stuck to the lid. Times spent at Vacation Bible School at Salvator Evangelical and Reformed Church linger in memory . . . as does the singing. Each year had a theme song. "Do You Know What Time It Is?" served that purpose one year. In high church terms, the song was an antiphon. With young children, it was more a contest over who could shout the refrain the loudest: "Do you know what time it is? TIME TO SERVE THE LORD!" I am sure there were other lines and verses, but I do not remember them. All that remains in my memory is the question and the answer.

Do you know what time it is?

References to time, especially hours, course through the Gospel of John. Initially, they relay the message of a time that is "not yet." *The hour is coming. His hour had not yet come.* Such times and hours are common to us, where the "not yet" involves some manner of waiting or preparation. Youth grow impatient for hours of independence to come to them. Persons and communities of faith offer prayers in hopes of understanding some situation still unfolding. We wait for an opportunity to take shape, knowing the right time for it has not yet arrived. Such hours teach us patience and the discipline of discernment. Ready or not, responsibilities do arrive; times for action and decision do appear. In the second chapter of John, Jesus declares to his mother prior to his first sign at Cana, "My hour has not yet come" (John 2:4). But times change, and hours come: *Jesus . . . looked up to heaven and said, "Father, the hour has come."*

People in many religious traditions pray according to the time of day. *Matins* and *vespers* recall such early monastic disciplines. Perhaps your own devotional schedule reflects a similar disposition to link particular times with prayers. Yet some times and hours cannot be marked by calendars or calibrated by watches. *Kairos*, a Greek word for "time," carries the connotation of an opportune moment. Jesus' hour of prayer just before betrayal is such a moment of *kairos*. Ministry and life itself hinge on the recognition of the opportune moment and on faithful response. Before Jesus prays anything else, he acknowledges that moment, the hour assigned him by God, has come.

Such hours come upon us as well. They are the times that decisively shape who we are, who we shall be, and what we shall do. They may be fleeting moments, brief opportunities or challenges arising in particular situations that may or may not come again. One crucial hour may call for extraordinary courage, another for honesty and forthrightness. A dire moment may force us to place our position, perhaps even our life, in harm's way for a greater cause or another person.

When such moments come, Jesus' prayer intends to transform our experience of the time at hand. *"Father, the hour has come."* We bring to God the great and the small in our lives, and we bring awareness of the presence and import of God in our hours of decisive turning and choosing. Why? To recognize and affirm that *all* our hours belong to and are lived in the presence of God. We experience God's presence in hours of calm and quiet. It should be no different when the hours turn critical and crucial. Timely prayer issues from the hours we face, whether they seem casual or pressing, routine or crisis.

Do you know what time it is? The songs of childhood sometimes teach us the deepest of lessons. Pray for and through each hour in which you live—today, now, at this very moment. For knowing the time may help you discern what God seeks for you in this hour.

Keep me sensitive to the timing of my prayer, O God: what hour it is in my life and in the life of your people and your world. In knowing the time, may I better use the time you give. Amen.

Spiritual Exercise

Write in your journal as much as you can remember of the previous hour in your life: activities, thoughts, opportunities. Afterward, prayerfully reflect on those moments. In what ways did the presence of God come to the forefront in the hour and as you look back now? Think of an "hour" approaching for you that involves a significant decision, action, and/or change on your part. Pray for God's leading and presence in that hour. Bring concerns or anxieties you have about that time into your prayer. Take a deep breath and give thanks for God's presence now. Exhale, and entrust that approaching time to God.

Day 3

GLORY BE

"Glorify me in your own presence
with the glory that I had in your presence
before the world existed."
—John 17:5

WHAT COMES TO YOUR mind and heart when you hear the word *glory*? An experience of God's majesty? fame or notoriety? a glimpse of heavenly realms? an act of praise? Given that range of understandings, what does it mean to glorify or to be glorified?

Jesus does not pray for glory and glorification out of a tradition unfamiliar with those terms. Jesus speaks and prays from his moorings in the Hebrew scriptures, particularly the narrative of God's redemption of Israel in Exodus. There, glory is not what differentiates God from the Israelites. Rather, glory is how and when God reveals God's own self and power in public ways for the sake of God's covenant partners.

Once the Israelites leave Egypt and enter the wilderness, they still require God's help and leading. Responding to God's promise of manna, Moses tells the Israelites, "In the morning you shall see the *glory* of the LORD" (Exod. 16:7, emphasis added). Guidance in the wilderness is a cloud that leads them by day: "and the *glory* of the LORD appeared in the cloud" (Exod. 16:10, emphasis added). God's glory in Exodus is manifested in God's choosing to act in visible ways to preserve life.

Similarly in John's Gospel, God's glory is to be revealed in yet another visible act of God's power exercised for the sake of giving life to God's people. A new "exodus" awaits the revelation of God's glory. Instead of parted seas, this new exodus will involve crossed timbers. God will once again be revealed.

Jesus prays to be glorified. His prayer does not arise from self-adulation. Glorification reveals God. Jesus' prayer is the opening of his life to the revealing of God's grace and love to the world. In that sense, glorification becomes the purpose of incarnation: to demonstrate and embody God among us.

God's glory gives us a new perspective not only upon the prayer of Jesus here, but upon how we would mirror its petition in our own lives. More than a few since James and John first pleaded for places of honor have mistaken the meaning of glorification. It is not about getting God's attention. It is about bearing witness to God.

The association of praise with glory is natural. When God becomes known to us in saving ways, praise results. But take careful note. Glory and praise are not necessarily synonyms. Jesus in this prayer does not merely say, "To God be the glory, great things he hath done!" Jesus offers his life as the means of God's glorification, no matter the cost. Our praise of Christ flows from the revelation of God in that sacrifice.

Would you be comfortable praying for God to glorify you? Humility might wince at that expression, thinking it too self-occupied. But remember: to be glorified involves vocation before it ever issues in congratulation. Our glory as human beings made in the image of God is to reveal God in creation, serving as instruments and conduits of Christ's love and grace, even when glorification comes cruciform.

A popular praise song these days contains this line: "In my life, Lord, be glorified." In the light of Jesus' prayer before betrayal, our lives should not simply praise God. The deeper meaning of glory invites our lives to *reveal* God. That is our glory as servants and friends of the One who so prayed.

Glorify me, O God: as Jesus prayed, so I pray. Not for my praise but for my service; not for my honor but for your revealing; not for others to see me but to see you in me. Amen.

Spiritual Exercise

Call to mind hymns or praise songs that have "glory" or "glorify" in their titles or verses. What do they convey to you about the revelation of God in life rather than simple praise. Pray aloud the first two words of Jesus' prayer from this reading (*"Glorify me"*) several times. Pause between each speaking of these words, prayerfully reflecting on how you might reveal God at home, work, school, or church. Listen in prayerful silence after each such reflection. Close with a prayer of thanks for the ways God has been revealed to you in this particular day. That is the glory of God entrusted to you!

Day 4

WHOSE WE ARE

*"They were yours, and you gave them to me, and they have kept
your word. Now they know that everything you have given me
is from you; for the words that you gave to me
I have given to them, and they have received them."*

—John 17:6-8

S EVERAL YEARS INTO my pastoral ministry, I attended a
regional luncheon for laity and clergy. Part of the program involved introducing ourselves to the gathering.
A pattern soon fell into place. Laity identified themselves by
church affiliation and either vocation or volunteer position in
the church. Clergy identified themselves as pastor of so-and-so
church and the name of the town. Clergy spouses, if not introduced by their husbands without opportunity to speak their
own names, identified themselves as the wife of pastor so-and-
so (at this time, all clergy spouses were wives). When my turn
came, I stood up and, perhaps hoping folks would pass off my
ill-mannered satire to youthful indiscretion, said, "My name is
John Indermark, and I am the husband of the pastor's wife in
Metaline Falls." To whom do you belong?

There is far more to Judy Indermark as a person and Christian than "my little wifey," as it seemed to me was the under-
current prevalent in the introductions that day. Even so,
belonging and identity do intertwine. In covenant relationships, we do belong to one another. Our identity does find explanation and expression in those with whom we join our lives
and hopes and commitments.

In Jesus' prayer in John 17, belonging and identity form part of Jesus' intercession. He acknowledges that he belongs to God: "Everything you have given me is from you." Jesus professes that his identity derives from God, that Jesus and God belong to each other. The identity of one, in Christian experience, becomes inseparable from the identity of the other. To speak of God requires speaking of Jesus, and vice versa.

Everything you have given me is from you. The same prayer that acknowledges Jesus' sense of belonging to God anticipates our own profession of providential grace. When we cast our perspective in wide angle across all that we have and all that we are and even all that we will be, God emerges as the constant in our lives as in Jesus' life. We belong, in Christ, to God. Who we are cannot be understood apart from *whose* we are.

Traveling the prayer paths of Jesus summons no small amount of humility. We do yearn sometimes to add to Jesus' words: *Everything you have given me is from you,* except for those things that I earned myself and belong to me, thank you. In relationships, we really do enjoy belonging to one another until demands are made that we can't abide. Then it's our way or the highway. We do that to one another. We do that to God. The story of the rich young ruler whom Jesus loved but allowed to walk away is not a once-in-a-millennia event. Belongings can get in the way when what we claim as our belongings becomes more important than to whom we belong. Sometimes we allow what we have to trump whose we are.

In Jesus' prayer, the clue to acting upon this sense of belonging to God comes in our disposition to a Word ("they have kept your word. . . . they have received [your words]"). In a Gospel whose opening declares that "the Word was with God, and the Word was God. . . . And the Word became flesh and lived among us," theology and prayer intersect. Words prayed and words lived yearn to speak about the Word to whom we belong.

Everything you have given me is from you. So Jesus prayed. So may we pray: in recognition of the providence of God that sustains us, in gratitude for the grace of God that receives us, in faithfulness to the Word of God that enters our lives. For in Christ, we belong to God.

When I have doubts about who I am or hope to be, help me, O God, to see you: in the Christ, in others, in word and sacrament. If I could but see you, I might truly see myself held in love, lifted in grace, blessed with hope. Amen.

Spiritual Exercise

Pray these words of Jesus aloud: *Everything you have given me is from you.* Each time you pray, emphasize a different word. Pause each time to reflect on the influence of each inflection in shaping the prayer's meaning. Journal your thoughts on the blessings, challenges, and opportunities God has given you at this moment in your life. Offer thanks for all God's gifts. Pray to discern what God might seek to do in your life through them. Close by repeating Jesus' words aloud. Entrust to God what you have entered in your journal.

Day 5

SAINT CHRISTOPHER

"Holy Father, protect them in your name. . . .
As you have sent me into the world,
so I have sent them into the world."
John 17:11,18

*I*N 1969 A BODY in the Roman Catholic Church, charged
with removing from sainthood those whose lives or
saintly acts had been deemed largely legendary, removed
Saint Christopher from the list of saints. He had been the patron saint of travelers. Whether in medallions worn around
necks or plastic statues affixed to the dashboards of cars, the
image of Saint Christopher had accompanied generations who
undertook journeys, whether measured in minutes or miles,
on pilgrimages routine as the store down the block or a once-
in-a-lifetime quest. Saint Christopher, so the legend goes, had
once borne a child on his back across a river. With each step
the man took, the child seemed to grow unexplainably heavier, until at last the weight pushed him under the water. He
then discovered the child was none other than Christ and the
submersion his baptism. From this legend emerged the man's
new name: Christopher, "Christ-bearer."

There are days and places today that make us long for the
reinstatement of a patron saint for travelers. Danger abounds.
Ask any victim of a violent crime. Ask a child who draws pictures of warfare, whether of the conventional sort or of drive-
by shootings in her own neighborhood from personal
memory. We begin to wonder whether Saint Christopher has

been too hastily dismissed. Legend or not, he at least reminded us of our need for someone to watch over us, someone to remember us when the trek turns perilous.

> *"Holy Father, protect them in your name. . . . While I was with them, I protected them in your name. . . . I am not asking you to take them out of the world, but I ask you to protect them. . . . As you have sent me into the world, so I have sent them into the world"* (John 17:11, 12, 15, 18).

Another patron saint of travelers voices this prayer for us. Jesus' prayer minces no words regarding our need for care and keeping. God's protection is invoked not once or twice but three times in this passage (John 17:11-18). Protection and insulation, however, are not synonyms. Christ's spirit runs counter to the rapturous expectation that faith will whisk us out of this world. Echoing off the walls of some long-lost upstairs room in Jerusalem comes faith's invitation and discipline: The journey is not out of this world but deep within it. Prayer simply, yet profoundly, becomes the journey's companion.

Of course, the journey would be easier if the way were safer, if we didn't have to venture too far, at least not into the night, at least not into *those* neighborhoods—be they geographical precincts, corners of the mind, or reaches of the heart we would prefer not having to travel. Not just now.

But there is a problem. God in Christ.

Jesus prays not only as patron of travelers but as our dispatcher. *As you have sent me into the world, so I have sent them into the world.* The One who intercedes for our protection is the One who gets us into those places where we need intercession in the first place. Grace can be a dangerous commodity to deal in, especially when it conflicts with the currency of "an eye for an eye" or "might makes right" or "you get what you deserve in life."

Holy Father, protect them. The way can get dicey. Dangers do abound, not because of an absence of faith but often as a direct result of it. But our trust in Jesus' prayer allows us to step out in faith and to continue stepping forward, even as the weight upon our shoulders becomes heavier. Christ holds us in prayer, even as we feel ourselves sinking. We are sent into the world to bear the weight and grace of Christ, to be Christ-bearers, to be Christophers. That is our baptism. So Jesus prays for those whom he sends. So may we pray as those sent.

Go in peace!

Form my life as a pilgrim's way, O God. I follow where Christ has already led, and I rely on you for life itself. Keep me in your care, no matter the circumstance. Amen.

Spiritual Exercise

Imagine yourself walking a familiar route you frequently take. Note the people you normally see, the scenes routinely observed. Ask yourself, *Where might I expect to encounter God on this route?* Plan on walking that way sometime this week. As you walk, pray silently for the persons you see along the way. Pray for God's keeping and protection of them on their journeys, known or unknown to you. Afterward, journal your thoughts and prayers from that trip. Reflect on how God might have been present to you. Pray tonight about your life's journey. Offer thanks for Christ's prayer for and presence with you on that journey.

Day 6

THE GENERATION CHURCH

"I ask not only on behalf of these,
but also on behalf of those who will believe in me
through their word, that they may all be one.
As you, Father, are in me and I am in you,
may they also be in us."

—John 17:20-21

HAT I KNOW about machines could be written in very large letters on a very small piece of paper. The functioning principles of generators were ably presented to me in grade-school science and just as ably forgotten. Even more removed from my direct knowledge or experience are the particulars of building such a machine. But I do remember standing in the production room at Seattle City Light's Boundary Dam in northeastern Washington and being amazed at the sight and literal sensation of those generators as they transformed the rush of water into a region's power source.

So what do generators in the northeast corner of Washington state have to do with the "generations" to which Jesus alludes here? Most of the time, generation refers either to a span of years or to the identity of a certain age group. The forty years of biblical generations compress these days as media speaks of Baby Boomers, generation Xers and Yers and other alphabet soup designations. There is certainly a sense today that Jesus' prayer addresses the "age-span" understanding of generations. Faith is generational, bridging diverse times.

But *generation* also brings to mind that which is generated, the result of activity, the fruit of labor, the tangible evidence of what has been produced and passed on. Faith is a "generation" of trust in God transformed into lives lived and witness kept. Faith's "generation" involves one group of disciples "generating" another. "I ask not only on behalf of these, but also on behalf of those who will believe in me *through their word*" (emphasis added). Jesus prays for generations of faith across generations.

Jesus prays for the unity of generations, *that they may all be one.* Too often the church settles for partisan visions of our mission, beleaguering and watering down institutional convictions until we arrive at a consensus that attempts to offend no one, and in the end excites the same number. Yet Jesus' prayer *that they may all be one* pushes our prayers and actions far deeper. The unity expressed there traces to the dynamic unity of God and Christ. *As you, Father, are in me and I am in you, may they also be in us.* The unity Jesus seeks in prayer is organic. It is unity whose nature is, to use a word sometimes demeaned by institutional architects but far more compelling in terms of its lived demands, *spiritual.* When was the last time you felt so connected to Christ's body in community that it seemed to you this must be what life and relationship are like with God and Christ? Such is the unity Jesus' and our prayers seek to generate.

And here we are, back at the beginning: *generations.* Unity with God in Christ serves as the intended generation of Jesus' prayer for his disciples, and of our prayers in its light, *so that the world may believe that you have sent me.* May our lives and witness generate the hope of our prayers.

Grant me those moments, O God, when I feel and experience union with you in Christ. May those moments generate in me the impetus to live in you ever more deeply. Amen.

Spiritual Exercise

Close your eyes and recall persons who played key roles in your coming to faith. What about their witness enabled you to grow spiritually? In your journal, reflect on your relationship with one of those persons. Relate what sense of unity you experienced with him or her at various points in the relationship. How did that experience of unity help you discern and know union with God? Offer a prayer of thanksgiving for the "generation" of faith between you and that individual. Reread John 17:20-21 with him or her in mind. Allow the scripture to affirm your "oneness" with that person, even now, in Christ.

Day 7

IN CHRIST = IN LOVE

" . . . so that the love with which you have loved me
may be in them, and I in them."
—John 17:26

*I*N LOVE." WHAT images or experiences does that phrase summon? Sometimes the phrase "in love" becomes a rationale for changed behavior: *What's wrong with Bill? I've never seen him so absentminded! / Oh, don't worry. He's just in love.* Sometimes it is a glib expression of an initial attraction not expected to lead anywhere, as in the tendency of some teenagers (and some elders!) to fall in and out of love with great frequency. More seriously, "in love" offers a benchmark to commitment: "I understand you want to marry my daughter. But are you really in love with her, or is this just an infatuation?"

The Gospel and Epistles of John focus at length on the meaning of love, frequently emphasizing love's revelation of God's nature: "God so loved the world" (John 3:16); "God is love" (1 John 4:8). Sometimes the emphasis shifts to love's ethical injunction commanded to those who would follow Jesus: "Love one another as I have loved you" (John 15:12); "Those who love God must love their brothers and sisters also" (1 John 4:21). Jesus closes his prayer to God in today's reading with the petition that the love of God may be "in them [us]" even as Christ remains "in them [us]." In other words, Jesus prays that we may dwell "in love" even as we live in Christ.

How often do you pray for that indwelling love for yourself, your congregation, or your family? How do your life and the lives of those for whom you pray evidence the fruits of such prayers, such love?

The conclusion of Jesus' prayer for his disciples offers a gracious gift and a demanding challenge: to live in Christ is to live in love. The church has occasionally been guilty of a somewhat flabby representation of the meaning of this challenge, relegating it to mere sentimentality or reducing it, as one preacher once said, to being good to Granny and not kicking the cat.

Love in the biblical witness, however, is not a matter of emotion or innocuous behavior. Love in action seeks another's good. When love comes in words spoken, it inevitably seeks words kept in deed. The love of God takes form in divine activity in response to and on behalf of that creation. The love of God explodes in the creation of the world. The love of God breaks out in exodus from Egypt. The love of God comes incarnate in a birth at Bethlehem and a death on Golgotha.

Dwelling in the love of the God revealed in Jesus Christ means embodying such love. The means and resources for doing so come in the love with which we are held by God in Christ that keeps love's command an act of grace. We are loved by God not so that we can sit in beatific delight at such a gift, but so that we can then love one another.

The call to live in love, and so to act with love, holds true even and especially when love does not find a ready welcome. We do not live in a world scripted by those who write and design greeting cards. God did not send the Beloved Child to a place entirely ready to receive the Christ. Even when we have the best of intentions, our efforts to love do not always succeed. Though hostility or apathy may be our natural inclination, though we may feel compelled to withhold our love in order to punish or instruct, Jesus' prayer commands us to dwell in love. Therefore, our prayers and actions should seek and reflect the grace and forgiveness of the love of God for and in us: *so that the love with which you have loved me may be in them, and I in them.*

In Christ, God has come to live in love with us. In Christ, may we come to live in love for others and for the One who so taught us.

Save me, O God, from cynical scorn of love or from a weak version of its call. As I live in you more deeply through Christ, may I grow in Christ to love more deeply. Amen.

Spiritual Exercise

Recall persons in your life who have told you they love you. Reflect on what those persons have done to reveal that love. Do the same exercise for those to whom you have spoken love. How have you translated your words of love into action? Journal what you experienced in this exercise (gratitude, regret, hope). Read John 17:26*b* aloud several times (*"so that the love . . ."*). With Jesus' prayer, and with those persons from the opening exercise in mind, pray to God in remembrance of those gifts of love, in confession of missed opportunities, in hopes of new possibilities to love. Close with thanks for God's love in Christ dwelling in you.

WEEK FIVE

At the Garden

Day 1

GARDENS, MAZES, AND LABYRINTHS

MATTHEW 26:36; MATTHEW 26:37, 38; LUKE 22:42;
MARK 14:37-38; LUKE 22:43-44; MATTHEW 26:46

*M*Y WIFE'S GRANDMOTHER WELTHA cultivated an extraordinary garden on her five acres in Corbett. From nursery catalogs, trips to England, and walkabouts in the Columbia Gorge, she collected a variety of seeds and starts that set down roots in long rows of flowers and tree-shaded beds with patches of color scattered here and there. When Judy first brought me to meet Granny, we went on a walking tour of her gardens. It did not take long to discern that the walk was part of the "liturgy" of any visit to what had at one time been a bulb and holly farm. Well-worn paths indicated that these circuits had been made over long years by children and grandchildren, visitors from abroad, and the good ladies of the Corbett Garden Club. For all I knew, this being my first visit, the course we followed out from the farmhouse, weaving in and out of the rows and back to the farmhouse, was the same for every visitor—a single course worn by countless footsteps of Weltha and her guests . . . a labyrinth.

I am told that the difference between a maze and a labyrinth, both of which have long associations with gardens, comes in a single distinction. A labyrinth is formed by a single path one follows in and then out. The path leads to a central point or "heart" through a series of "circuits," with no choices to confuse or trick along the way. If there were, it would not be a labyrinth but a maze. You have only one choice when facing a labyrinth: to enter or not. I would add a second option: either complete the circuits by arriving at the heart or turn back beforehand.

Gardens for many persons evoke reflection, which makes them ideal settings for labyrinths. In the sights, sounds, smells, sensations of touch, and even taste available in a garden, a person can easily immerse himself or herself in the cycle of life, death, and rebirth that forms the basis for any self-sustaining garden. Mulch and decay belong as much to the garden as do blooms and photosynthesis. Walking a labyrinth invites contemplation of that cycle in our own lives.

Through this week's readings, you will enter a garden with Jesus. Two of the Gospels name the place as Gethsemane, whose meaning is "oil press." The garden may actually have been a grove or orchard. If the dating of Holy Week to the first week of April is true, the trees may or may not have yet budded, as the olive flowers generally do not appear until May. Residual smells of the olive fruit pressed in December or later might still linger on the stone presses from which the garden took its name.

Jesus and the disciples who accompany him do not journey to Gethsemane to marvel at the beauties of creation found in a garden. For Jesus, and as he encourages those who enter with him to see it, the garden provides a place for prayer. Gethsemane confronts them all with the spiritual counterpart of both a maze and a labyrinth.

In a maze, you never know if a path represents the way through or a dead-end—or worse yet, a deeper penetration that leads to a series of choices, all eventually going nowhere except to greater confusion. Gethsemane's maze consists of the multiple choices bewildering teacher and followers, driving the former to excruciating prayer and the latter to sleep: *What way shall we take? What response shall we make to those who will join us with torches, clubs, and swords? What options remain?* Do not rush to judgment against disciples who close their eyes to this garden's darkness. Prayer does not always come easily. In this garden, it comes with struggle and agony even to the One who teaches us to pray.

Yet through the prayers of Jesus in these readings we discover that what confronts him is less a maze than a labyrinth. For some time, the narrative of Jesus' ministry has followed a single direction, a single path that leads to Jerusalem . . . and now to this garden. The scent of decaying leaves and rotted olives left on the ground from the harvest may heighten the realization of what looms ahead on the path so long taken: a single path and the only choice after entry is whether to continue or turn around before reaching the dark heart of this labyrinth. *My Father, if it be possible, let this cup pass from me.* The heart of this labyrinth is not to be taken lightly.

You and I do not have the benefit of walking this circuit through Gethsemane's garden with Jesus. We do, however, have the stories and the discipline of prayer. We can reflect upon the intersection between these stories and our lives. Indeed, prayer can become our means of walking Gethsemane's labyrinth. In doing so, prayer can help us discern what resides at the core of our journey in faith, and whether we will choose to enter and complete this path wherever it leads.

It may seem that this garden labyrinth holds no surprises. We have been this way before, at least in the seasonal repetitions of Jesus' passion narrative. But that familiarity is the beauty and power of gardens. Each time we walk their circuits with senses open, new and old, dying and living mingle to bring a fresh experience of life unfolding all around. Each time we walk Gethsemane's circuit with spirit open to words new and old; themes of dying and rising mingle to bring a fresh experience of grace birthing deep within.

The gate of Gethsemane's labyrinth swings open before you. The choice is yours.

Walk beside me, O God, for I need your presence. Walk behind me, Spirit, lest I fall or turn back. Walk before me, O Christ, for it is you I would follow on the way. Amen.

Spiritual Exercise

This week, find a garden or park in which to walk or otherwise traverse. As you walk, take in the sights, smells, sounds, and touches of that place. Seek in each sensation a hint or gift of God brought to that place, perhaps even to you. Use some of your time there to reflect on your journey with God at this juncture in your life. Be attentive to how God may be calling or leading you in some new way or direction. In your journal, record your thoughts in that place, particularly those reflections upon God's presence and calling in your life. Offer a prayer of thanks for the gift of places where you find your spirit nourished.

Day 2

HERE AND THERE

"Sit here while I go over there and pray."
—Matthew 26:36

*H*ERE AND THERE. What is the distance between those two points? A heartbeat? A chasm? It all depends on where you happen to be standing—or praying.

According to Matthew, as Jesus enters the garden of Gethsemane with his disciples, he offers this word of instruction that establishes an initial separation between rabbi and learners, between pray-er and watch-ers: "Sit here while I go over there." Luke offers a graphic detail to describe the distance between this particular "here and there": about a stone's throw. Similar expressions occur in other ancient writings: a javelin's throw away (Thucydides) or a bowshot (Gen. 21:15). In a military sense, such a distance connotes a sense of safety from danger (that is, outside of a weapon's range). Jesus separates himself from his disciples, though whether for their safety or his privacy the accounts do not say. Matthew, Mark, and Luke agree, however, on the reality of a distance involved: *Sit here while I go . . . there.*

Consider the effect of distance on personal relationships. A couple finds their relationship falling apart, a widening separation in emotional presence or attachment. "You're never here for me." And the difference between "here" and "there" in that instance need not be defined by geographical isolation. Two people may face each other across the table every day, yet never be "there" for each other.

Being "here" requires attention to presence, needs, and hopes. "Being here for me" involves taking the time and vulnerability to open your life to mine.

So it is with human relationships. So it is in the garden. While "here"and "there" enter the scene as Jesus' instructions, those words become an ominous clue to the crisis soon to unfold. Disciples not "there" with Jesus in prayer become those not "there" with him in trial or judgment or execution.

The disciplines of spiritual formation invite a commitment to presence, to being "here" to God's spirit as well as to one another. In modern usage, the phrase "here and there" suggests a state of scattering, of things (or persons) dotting a landscape but having no clear connection or tie. Prayer and devotional life can fall into such a state of disconnection. Our spirits and minds lose focus. We drift and wander. We fall asleep, physically or spiritually. Have you ever been in a conversation only to realize you have not been listening, *really* listening, to what the person has been saying or meaning? We can find ourselves "here and there" in such situations, losing connection with or awareness of the one to whom we speak or listen—or the One to whom we pray.

Sit here while I go there. As ensuing readings will underscore, Jesus' prayer in the garden moves into an intensely personal encounter with God. The assignation of "here" and "there" may be inevitable in this circumstance—and at times in our own. Some prayers and encounters we enter in solitude. But "solitude" and "isolation" are not synonymous. In solitude, community can still surround and support. Our inability to go where another's spiritual journey leads does not mean we cannot support from a distance. In bringing the disciples with him to the garden Jesus remains open to the potential gift of community.

Sit here while I go there. Jesus teaches prayer that disciplines us to place. God has a purpose in calling us to where we are.

Faithfulness in those moments comes in remaining open to the Spirit's movement, in committing ourselves to be present to God and to the one with whom we would stand or sit—and the One to whom we pray.

God of holy presence, you are always here for me. By your Spirit's leading, may I likewise be there for those who need me—and you. Help me be one through whom you would be there. Amen.

Spiritual Exercise

Imagine yourself in the garden with Jesus and the disciples. When Jesus tells you to *sit here while I go over there,* what do you pray for Jesus, for the disciples, and for yourself? In your journal, record those prayers and thoughts. Afterward, read them over. What do they reveal about your faith, life, or relationship with Christ? Reflect on one person for whom it would be important for you to be "there" in the coming day or week. List ways in which you might do that and how those ways spring not only from your relationship with that person but from your relationship with God. Offer a prayer of thanks for God's presence. Open yourself that God may touch others through you.

Day 3

AWAKE TO COMPASSION

[Jesus] took with him Peter and the two sons of Zebedee
[James and John], . . . "Remain here, and stay awake with me."
—Matthew 26:37, 38

WHAT IF? As a youth, I once came across a book whose title (I believe) was: *If the South Had Won the Civil War.* Though I have long since forgotten the details, the author conjectured on the results had several key battles gone the other way and delivered a Confederate victory. Projected changes in political, economic, and social life in a now-divided nation dominated the small volume. Of course, that is not how history turned out. But what if?

Jesus does not seek complete solitude in the garden. Even after charging the disciples to "sit here while I go over there," Jesus singles out three to accompany him further, not only in distance but in emotion and responsibility. An invitation to community comes in words of remarkable vulnerability joined to a simple request. Will it be accepted?

I am deeply grieved, even to death . . . stay awake with me. Some styles of leadership avoid any admission of weakness or vulnerability. Don't let your guard down. Don't let your enemies, much less your friends, know your true feelings. Not here.

Just a few chapters prior in Matthew, two of the three disciples whom Jesus invites now into this community of wakefulness had generated a turmoil among the others by bringing to Jesus their mother's request for places of honor for them in the kingdom. The other ten were indignant, though whether at the request or not having made it themselves first Matthew does not say. The Gospel does record Jesus' contrasting the world's way of greatness (leadership) with the true greatness of those who would follow his way. "Lording it over"—maintaining control at any cost—belongs to the past. The future belongs to those people who are open to and accepting of the vulnerability of servanthood.

But what does such leadership look like? One example comes in the gardened invitation to join Jesus in prayerful community: a community that fully recognizes the agony of the moment and commits to "staying awake" to the One in need. In that invitation, in the potential of that community, Jesus enacts the reversal of greatness and service once talked about. Remember who is grieved unto death and who is invited to stand by that one. Jesus makes himself vulnerable, inviting the wakefulness and prayers of the disciples for him.

That brings us back to our opening question: What if? What if Peter, James, and John had kept vigil? What if they had shared Jesus' suffering (passion) in that moment, sustaining him with a community of com-passion ("suffering with")? Would they later have fled into the night? Would all but one have left it to the women alone to keep vigil at the cross?

We might argue that "what if" doesn't matter, because we know what happened. We know the invitation to community lapsed into sleep. That's history but not the end of the story.

The invitation remains. Jesus' entering into prayer at Gethsemane invokes this invitation to community, and the invitation remains for us. We still enter those places where we can imagine Jesus' being grieved unto death: at the death of innocents, in the frustrating search for peace amid violence, in the hard realities of starvation and homelessness among God's children. And when we enter those places, Jesus still beckons us to community, community that shares the suffering and stays awake to the needs (and causes!) immediate to us rather than doze off in indifference or callousness.

Such a community beckons us to prayer in lively, at times painful, solidarity with this world. For we know where we will find Jesus: in the heart of suffering. And we know where Jesus would lead us: into acts of sacrificial servanthood. Gethsemane's invitation remains. What if . . . what if I become a person in a community awake to com-passion?

Stay awake with me!

We are grateful, O God, for the rest you bring to us for renewal and for the wakefulness to which you summon us in order to embody that renewal in prayer and service. Amen.

Spiritual Exercise

Choose a time when it may be difficult to concentrate or one in which you do not normally pray or engage in devotional practices. Call to mind a single person, group, or situation that you feel grieves Jesus. Pray for that person/group/situation from different angles: from your knowledge, from your imagining of what the need may be, from your belief in God's hopes for that need, from your frustration at not knowing why the need exists. Afterward, journal your thoughts about this prayer: its ease, its struggle, your experience of God's presence and leading.

Day 4

GOD WILLING, MY WILLING

"Father, if you are willing, remove this cup from me;
yet, not my will but yours be done."
—Luke 22:42

*I*T WAS GOD'S WILL. How many times have you heard those words solemnly intoned or offered them yourself? Moments of unexplainable tragedy seem to give those words their most frequent venting. A natural disaster unleashes itself unannounced on unsuspecting victims. A human disaster generated by violence, random or pinpoint, claims innocents. An infant dies of SIDS. An elder loses mind and personality to Alzheimer's. When we can summon no other explanation or rationalization or comfort, God's will becomes the fall-back position. God's will brings order to chaos, divine purposefulness to experience. There has to be a reason. Right?

Jesus' prayer in the garden of Gethsemane takes a different course. The search for God's will there does not move backward in time, seeking some satisfactory resolution as to why bad things happen to good people. In the garden, the will of God to which Jesus addresses himself, and eventually entrusts himself, encompasses what is yet to be.

Father, if you are willing . . . An intriguing conversation goes on in some quarters of the church today: Does God know and therefore will every future action, or does human free will create some variation in what may yet be? Proponents of "open theism" hold some degree of openness to God's allowing human choice to shape the future. Where would you place yourself in that conversation? More importantly, how does your understanding influence the way you seek to live in obedience to, or pray for discernment of, the will of God?

Father, if you are willing . . . In the garden, Jesus prays to the God whom he understands may be "willing" to consider another possibility than the one gathering steam ever since he took the road to Jerusalem. If choice does not exist, Jesus' prayer is nonsensical. Why badger God with requests that can never be?

From there, the prayer moves to an extraordinary glimpse of Jesus' humanity, perhaps only equaled in his prayer-cry of forsakenness on the cross. Within the will of God, Jesus seeks movement, the possibility of another way: *Remove this cup from me.* These are not casual words. They arise from a spirit deeply rooted in honesty before God. Jesus takes the will (as in willingness) of God to heart and prayer, baring his spirit's yearning in hopes of another way to be taken.

Yet, not my will but yours be done. Listen to those words again. *Not my will but yours.* Unless Jesus simply mouths them for effect, they suggest a will in him at variance with the one that grows more imminent and ominous as this night deepens. Jesus' prayer does not gloss over the differences between "my" and "yours." There is tension between them as well as trust. Even with the hope of another way, even with the possibility that this cup might not have to be lifted, Jesus entrusts himself prayerfully, "will-fully," to the One he has come to reveal.

Jesus models an extraordinary act of prayer for those who would pray in his example. In his willingness to address God's willing, we find the encouragement to seek out in prayer the will of God, not as a static and immovable determination of what must be but as doors God might open to what could be. Jesus' compelling honesty and openness before God challenges us to pray from the depths of the heart, where questions may not have answers and where several degrees of separation may lie between our wills and God's will. In Jesus' willingness to trust God even when the answers do not fall his way, we discover the potential of prayer to guide and sustain us as we entrust ourselves to greater purposes than our minds and interests can conceive.

Not my will but yours be done. To pray so is to begin to live so.

God of majesty and mystery, do I even begin to know the fullness of your purpose and will for all things? No. But I know you can be trusted, for I have heard Jesus pray. Teach me to pray likewise. Amen.

Spiritual Exercise

In your journal, write about an experience where God's will was used or claimed in a way that troubled you. What caused your concern? How is your understanding of God's will different now from then? How has that change in understanding influenced (or been shaped by) your prayer life? Pray Jesus' words in Luke 22:42 as your own prayer. What cup comes to mind that you would have removed? Pray the words again, naming your cup. Be silent. Pray aloud the final words again: "Yet, not my will but yours be done." Own those words.

Day 5

SPIRIT AND BODY

He came and found them sleeping. . . .
"The spirit indeed is willing, but the flesh is weak."
—Mark 14:37-38

*A*N ANCIENT HERESY in the church known as Docetism cultivated an extreme separation between spirit and body. Spirit belonged to God and to life lived in God. Body belonged to physical existence, to life separated from God. Jesus only "appeared" to have a body (hence the name of the movement, whose title in Greek means "to seem"). For Docetists, spiritual life consisted of deadening self to the influence of the body to become "spiritual" persons.

In the garden, Jesus distinguishes between spirit and body (flesh). The former is willing ("eager" could also translate that word), the latter is weak. But notice that Jesus does not say the flesh is hopeless or utterly depraved or to be jettisoned in order to achieve a purely spiritual existence in the realm of the divine. No, Jesus just says the body is weak. And all the willing spirit in the world won't open weakened eyes.

So why include today's narrative in a book on Jesus' prayers? Jesus isn't praying here, and clearly the disciples are not. But that's the point. In a rather candid way, Jesus teaches about prayer, as well as spiritual formation. That teaching has to do with the unity of spirit and body in human existence and spiritual growth. In the words of the old song, "You can't have one without the other." God created us as persons of body *and* spirit.

Unconsciously, we teach this interconnectedness of body and spirit to the youngest of our children. I remember the instructions for prayer in the opening exercises of the primary department at Salvator E & R Church. You may recall similar lessons. Were we told just to set our spirits on God? No. We were told to fold our hands and close our eyes. Someone spoke. Others listened. To engage the spirit, we engage the body. The caution comes in not making that process mechanical ("You can't pray unless you follow all the steps in order") or magical ("If I sneak a peak and barely open my eyes, I might catch a glimpse of God, who only shows up when I'm not looking"). But what we teach our children still holds true for us as adults (as it did for disciples in the garden): Prayer and spirituality involve body and spirit in tandem, not opposition.

The problem Jesus confronts and names in the garden is inattentiveness, weakness in body. In the disciples' defense, it is late at night. People do need to sleep. That provides a purely physical explanation for a purely physical (body) problem. However, the disciples' "bodies" have become disengaged precisely because of their waning spirits. Spirits eager to profess devotion stay alert no matter what comes, but spirits reluctant to admit, much less accept, a suffering messiah may ebb. Spirits eager to have places of honor in God's realm stay energized, but spirits averse to taking a stand in the high priest's courtyard or at the foot of a cross may fade. Discipleship, prayer, faith: None can make it on body or spirit alone. God fashioned us as whole persons, spirit and body.

Jesus' words in the garden speak to our practices of prayer: not only in prayer's concern for others' and our physical existence but in the very expressions we use in prayer. Prayer, our communing with God in spirit, seeks bodily expression. Sometimes that expression reflects tradition and habit: folded hands or closed eyes, knees bent or hands uplifted. Those of us from different traditions may feel various degrees of comfort with some prayer expressions, so we differ in the postures and gestures we use in prayer. Yet those postures and gestures help us remember that we pray with our whole selves to God. Physical abilities and challenges may change over time and circumstance. How we bring our body into prayer may require adjustment. But God has fashioned us as persons united in spirit and body.

The spirit is indeed willing, but the flesh is weak. Jesus seeks prayer rooted in the whole of our being, body and spirit. That is how Jesus came among us, and that is who we are.

Help me, O God, to value my creation as a unity of body and spirit. Enable me to nurture those gifts, that both may offer my praise and seek your purposes. Amen.

Spiritual Exercise

Spend a few moments considering the ways your prayer practices involve your body (posture, gestures). Journal those observations. You may actually need to engage in prayer to see what it is you do. Afterward, reflect on the connection of those bodily expressions to your prayers. What do they convey to God? to you? Ask a willing and trusted person to watch as you pray, looking for ways you involve your body in prayer. Listen to what he or she observed. Offer a prayer of thanks for the marvelous way God has knit you together in spirit and body.

Day 6

PRAYER AS GRACE AND LABOR

*Then an angel from heaven appeared to him and gave him strength.
In his anguish he prayed more earnestly, and his sweat
became like great drops of blood.*

—Luke 22:43-44

GENESIS NARRATES the story of Jacob wrestling with a stranger through the night, a stranger strongly hinted to be God. That story's closest parallel comes in Jesus' prayer in Gethsemane. *Anguish* in the garden's narrative translates the Greek word *agonia*, from which we derive the English word *agony*. The Greek word suggests broader meanings involving struggle or the effort required in an athletic contest.

In Gethsemane, Jesus prays in *agonia*—struggle, labor, intensity, anguish. The depth of that effort finds further expression in an extraordinary metaphor: *His sweat became like great drops of blood*. Popular piety has sometimes commandeered that image to insist on a literal miracle of Jesus' sweating blood. But the text says *like*. In Luke's use of symbolic language, Jesus' perspiration falls to the ground the way blood might bead and drip. The imagery of blood ties Gethsemane to Golgotha.

Jesus' sweat ties his prayer to intense labor. Physical exertion activates the body's built-in cooling system, common to every human being. We expect sweat to pour off a laborer in the field under the sun, even a carpenter working at a bench in a stuffy workroom. But the image of a rabbi in the cool of night in the shade of trees, drenched in sweat from prayer, is unexpected.

Before the labor, before the *agonia* of Jesus' prayer comes the grace of God: "Then an angel from heaven appeared to him and gave him strength." This is not the first time an angel has come to Jesus' aid. Following his temptation in the wilderness, both Matthew and Mark record that angels "wait on" (minister to) Jesus. That ministering presence comes *after* the struggle with temptation, as if to replenish stores used in confronting the tempter. In the garden, the grace of a ministering angel comes before this immersion in the labor and intensity of prayer, as if to provide the strength needed for such prayer.

Grace and labor came together in Jesus' Gethsemane prayer. They still may for us.

All prayer to some degree involves effort, but the labor of Jesus' prayer seems extraordinary. How can one pray so fervently and intensely with body and spirit joined so closely that sweat pours while petitions soar? How can we possibly mirror such prayer? If such questions come to you, keep two things in mind.

First, Luke's narrative of Jesus' prayer in the garden is unique; the intense labor does not accompany every account of Jesus' prayer. We may not "sweat like blood falling to the ground" every time we approach God in prayer, but such times may come in the most severe circumstances: the bedside vigil for a child, grappling with the news of a terminal diagnosis for oneself or one's partner. Perhaps you already know the intensity of prayers such moments evoke.

When you do face such *agonia* in prayer, remember the second thing about Jesus' garden prayer: the presence and gift of God's grace to strengthen in order to pray. God's angelic presence prepared and sustained Jesus through Gethsemane's prayer. Likewise, God's grace will prepare and sustain you through prayers that take you to the depths of life and death. You do not go alone or unaided. God will be with you. So you may pray. So you may live. So you may hope.

When I am weary and without words, be with me, O God. Strengthen me with your grace for my labors and my prayers. Sustain me by your presence. Amen.

Spiritual Exercise

Recall some experience where you labored in prayer. What kept you at prayer? How did that prayer affect you physically? Where and how did you experience the grace of renewal in its wake? In your journal, make note of these reflections. Read through them, and then read Luke 22:43-44. In what ways was your prayer experience like that of Jesus in the garden? Offer a prayer of thanks for the experience of God strengthening you for prayer in ordinary and extraordinary times.

Day 7

LEAVING THE SANCTUARY

"Get up, let us be going."
—Matthew 26:45

G IDDYUP!" I AM NOT a horseman. Outside of mutually
suspicious encounters with equines at Boy Scout Camp S
Bar F in Missouri and trail rides out of Roosevelt
Lodge at Yellowstone National Park, I have tended to steer clear
of stallions and mares. However, I did watch Hopalong Cassidy
in my youth. And I do recall that one of the equivalents to stepping on the gas pedal of more familiar forms of transportation
to me was a shouted "giddyup!" With that command, a steed at
rest, or even balking, could be set to fly at a full gallop. I am sure
getting horses to take off is much more complicated than the
1950s Saturday morning westerns made it to be.

Whether with horses or people, catching attention, breaking inertia, and getting things moving sometimes means shout-
ing the equivalent of "Giddyup!" That's an unusual expression.
If you break it down, it sounds as if its derivation is "Get ye up!"

Get up, let us be going. So Jesus summons the disciples in the
garden. He speaks the words when his prayers and their slum-
bers have reached their conclusion. As much as the disciples
might have wished to remain asleep and Jesus to remain in
prayer, those times have passed. Betrayal and betrayer draw
near. "Get ye up!"

The garden of Gethsemane has served as a sanctuary for
both Jesus and the disciples. For Jesus, the sanctuary has offered

encounter with God in intense prayer. For the disciples, it has taken shape in a sleepy escape from words and fears, growing ever more ominous in Jerusalem. Lest we criticize the disciples too harshly, we need to recall occasions when we have sought in worship or devotion a place of escape, of retreat, of insulation from a painful and confusing world. On our better and stronger days, keeping vigil as did Jesus would be our preference and hope. But on other days, vigilance may be far removed from what we seek or bring to sanctuary. So it was for those disciples at Gethsemane.

But for Jesus and those disciples, as well as for you and me, sanctuary is not where life unwinds and faith unfolds. To disciples then and now who might prefer to remain in peaceful but disengaged sleep and to others then and now who might prefer to immerse themselves in profound but isolated prayer, Jesus announces: Time's up. Life's ahead. Get ye up!

The closing words of Jesus' prayer in the garden are not "Amen" but "Let us be going." They are the benediction to the garden's sanctuary, the commissioning to the road now to be taken: by Jesus, by those disciples, and by us. Prayer's measure does not come in the eloquence of words or loftiness of thoughts or earnestness of spirit. Prayer's measure comes in what happens after knees unbend, hands unfold, eyes open, and the door to closet or sanctuary swings wide open, bringing the world into full and confounding view. The garden prayer's close insists that prayer inevitably, graciously, and purposefully boots us out of the sanctuary.

Experiencing the presence of God and practicing spiritual disciplines rely on that same movement: knowing when it is time to leave the sanctuary, knowing when Christ summons us to be up and going. Someone once noted that church doors should swing in both directions to remind us that getting out is as important as getting in. In spiritual formation, practices and disciplines that draw us closer to God need to swing both ways, reminding us that a closer walk with God inevitably commissions us to a new way of living in this world.

So go in the blessing of Jesus' benediction: *Get up, let us be going.* Go with God.

I pray, O God, for moments when I may be in your presence and feast on your grace. Then send me, having been so fed, out the door and on your way. In Jesus Christ. Amen.

Spiritual Exercise

Think of a time in your spiritual journey when you have gone somewhere, literally or spiritually, you did not want to go. Write about that experience in your journal, using these questions for guidance: What required or led you to go there? In what ways did you experience God in the sending? What did you learn about God, yourself, and your faith in that place? Read over your notes, and then read Matthew 26:36-46. How was your experience similar to that of Jesus and his disciples in Gethsemane? In your experience with whom do you identify more—Jesus or the disciples? Why? Reread verse 46. Where do you see God leading you now?

WEEK SIX

Upon the Cross

Day 1

CROSS WORDS

LUKE 23:34; MATTHEW 27:46; MARK 15:30, 32;
JOHN 19:28; JOHN 19:30; LUKE 23:46

O, but they say the tongues of dying men
Enforce attention like deep harmony;
Where words are scarce, they are seldom spent in vain,
For they breathe truth that breathe their words in pain.
—Shakespeare, *King Richard II*, 2.1.5–8

*T*he OXFORD BOOK *of Death*, a collection of poems and stories, reflections and anecdotes about death, nestles on one of the shelves in my home library. Its chapters cover themes ranging from "The Hour of Death" to "Mourning" to "Children" to "Hereafters." The final chapter includes "last words" attributed to persons in their dying moments.

Headlining that final chapter is the above quote from Shakespeare. Its final two lines are sometimes grossly parodied in overly dramatic passages in literature and films, where whispered deathbed words resolve otherwise inexplicable riddles or right long-borne wrongs. Yet such parodies would not even be attempted were it not for a deep-seated human inclination to accept the witness of Shakespeare's lines: Final words are important. Human nature tends to accept a person's final utterances as genuine. We would at least grant that those words reveal something of the individual's true nature and character.

Put yourself in that position. If you knew yourself to be

dying and had but a few breaths with which to form words, what would you say? What would be your last testimony about this life or your relationships in it? Would you speak of things secondary, tangential? Or would you summon your final energy to speak from the depths of heart, mind, and spirit?

The issue of final words awaits a time over which we have little control, but in this concluding chapter we take our place before Jesus' cross and listen to his choice of final words and prayers. For on the cross, as in life, Jesus remains in conversation with God.

In this book's first reading, I offered a definition of prayer from the church tradition in which I was raised: Prayer is the conversation of the heart with God. The cross reveals that heartfelt conversation in stark relief, illuminating the character of Jesus' life by what forms his prayers in dying. The cross and Jesus' prayers upon it (and one he does not offer!) return us to the core of Jesus' ministry and revelation of God: forgiveness and intimacy with God, the prerogative of his divine nature and his sharing of human nature, the very purposes of Jesus' coming—all find themselves not only tested by but engaged through cross words offered as cross prayers.

This final chapter's readings will not include all the words Jesus speaks from the cross, sometimes called collectively "The Seven Last Words." Not all those words are prayers, but that in no way minimizes the importance of the others. In fact, two sets of words might well be interpreted as answers to prayers.

In the first set, Jesus declares to his mother Mary and the disciple standing beside her: "Woman, here is your son" and "Here is your mother" (John 19:26, 27). As the eldest child in the family, Jesus would have been responsible for the care of a widowed mother. Even now in his dying, he does not neglect that very human and poignant charge. The disciple to whom Jesus entrusts the care of his mother (and implicitly vice versa) is "the disciple whom [Jesus] loved," that is, the disciple who might likely feel the greatest grief at Jesus' death. Both mother and disciple (whom tradition holds to be John) find their needs, if not prayers, responded to through Jesus' last words.

The other set of words is Jesus' response to a plea from one of the condemned criminals: "Jesus, remember me when you come into your kingdom" finds answer in "Truly I tell you, today you will be with me in Paradise" (Luke 23:42,43). Again, Jesus does not offer his words as a prayer, but clearly they come in response to the words of another that were perhaps as close as the criminal could come to prayer.

So even in these words offered to Mary and John and Dismas (as tradition has remembered the name of the thief on the cross), prayer looms in the background. In his dying, in his final words, Jesus opens himself to the needs and petitions of others for community, love, and remembrance. As Jesus has lived in openness to human need, so Jesus dies.

But what does all of this have to do with us? This journey into Jesus' prayers invites a reshaping and renewing of our own practice of prayer. At the intersection of life and death that is the cross, relationships and values, faith and prayers find their ultimate testing. When we come before the foot of the cross and see in Jesus' dying our own mortality, the question becomes, how shall we *now* live and pray? How shall we pray in moments of opportunity and crisis in light of Jesus' prayers? How shall we form our present words to God, so that final words may flow seamlessly and with integrity?

> Where words are scarce, they are seldom spent in vain,
> For they breathe truth that breathe their words in pain.

So Jesus spoke and prayed on the cross. So may we learn to pray as Jesus prayed, that we may learn to live and die as well.

Before I encounter my time for final words, O God, help me to listen, speak, and pray with faith and grace in these present times and to entrust that later time to you. Amen.

Spiritual Exercise

Imagine you have learned that death will come to you this very night. In your journal, write what you would want your last words to be and to whom you would speak them. Limit yourself to no more than five sentences. Read over what you have written. What does it say about your relationships and priorities? What does it say about your faith? What does it say about your life and practice of prayer? Offer a prayer of gratitude for the gift of life and for the time you have been given to speak and pray about what is important. If any of your imagined last words would be helpful for others to hear, make a point of speaking to them in the next day or so.

Day 2

Not by Word Alone

"Father, forgive them; for they do not know what they are doing."
—Luke 23:34

ON THE DAY I BEGAN to write these words, a community in my state gathered to mourn the death of an eight-year-old boy, allegedly beaten to death by a teenage neighbor. I can scarcely imagine what must be filling the hearts of the dead child's parents and siblings today—extraordinary loss, unspeakable sorrow.

And of all the thoughts and prayers filling that sanctuary on a sunny April afternoon, what of those for the boy who will be charged with the murder? What will be sought for the youth whose bare hands carried out what brings a family and a community to its knees?

If it had been my child, I would not want some outsider telling me I have to forgive. I would not trust a pastor (or writer) who tells me that my Christian duty is to go to the courthouse and tell the defendant, "I forgive you," even if couched in the persuasive language of therapy and "getting on with your life by not carrying this inside you." Not yet. Not while I still hear the echoes of my child's blood crying from the ground (Gen. 4:10).

In the first prayer of Jesus from the cross, we hear this most unlikely petition: *Father, forgive them; for they do not know what they are doing.* Remember for whom Jesus offers this prayer: not people who fail to tithe or regularly miss Sunday worship, not even for the folks who will soon show up beneath the cross and speak unkind things. Jesus prays for those whose hands have driven nails, whose arms and backs have lifted the killing timbers into place, whose lies and plottings have put him on that hill. Jesus prays for those who kill him.

The prayer seems so, well, out of place. Forgiveness is not the word or prayer we might have expected to hear first. Perhaps when all is over and done, when regret and disgust replace carrying out orders and mocking. Perhaps then, if at all. But to forgive at the beginning? How does one even consider forgiveness in such a place, in such a time?

Yet Jesus calls upon God as Father to forgive those who gather to kill the Beloved Son. Consider carefully the import of that detail. The prayer does not record Jesus' bestowing forgiveness, but his calling upon God to forgive. It is one thing to forgive those who harm you but quite another to forgive someone who hurts someone whom you love.

Jesus does not offer his own forgiveness to the crucifiers in this prayer. Far more profoundly and perhaps far more for our sake, he calls upon God to grant forgiveness: God the Father, the aggrieved parent. Forgive them. Forgive those who cause suffering even unto death to the one you love. Why do I say for our sake? Occasionally we may find ourselves unable to forgive another. But in Christ's example we can take the first step, tentative as it may be, by invoking God's forgiveness. Might asking God's forgiveness of another when we cannot be an act of seeking God's grace to intervene for us? to prepare us for the time when we can forgive?

Father, forgive them. May we pray as Jesus prayed, that in time we may find the grace to live as Jesus lived.

Father, forgive them. *You know who "they" are in my life, O God. You know whom I have difficulty forgiving, and why. Forgive them, O Lord, and thus sows seeds of forgiveness in me. Amen.*

Spiritual Exercise

Reread the opening paragraphs. What difficult experiences of your own forgiveness of others do they summon? Be at prayer about your personal struggles with forgiveness. In your journal, make note of what you find most difficult to forgive in others and of any thoughts as to why. Offer Jesus' prayer as your own for one such struggle you have in forgiving another. Allow the gift of asking God's forgiveness for that person to help you move past resentments and even the desire for retribution and to take a step closer to forgiving.

Day 3

HONEST TO GOD

"My God, my God, why have you forsaken me?"
—Matthew 27:46

*F*ORSAKE. ABANDON. Leave. Desert. These are not the
typical verbs encountered in the prayers of the faithful, at least not in reference to the [in]activity of God
in our lives. Yet that is what Jesus prays to God upon the cross
—why have you forsaken me?

Our prayers to God do not always come freshly imagined
and newly formed from our hearts alone. We pray as we believe: from within a tradition. Sometimes when our own words
fail us, the words of the tradition with which we have grown
up come to mind and heart: the line of a hymn, the phrase of
a creed, the glimmer of a long-forgotten prayer, a verse of
scripture from childhood.

Tradition is at work with this prayer of Jesus. Six agonizing
hours, hours of separation from human compassion, hours of
descent into darkness and pain spell out the trauma of God-
forsakenness. How does one cry out such an experience? What
words can possibly express such an unbearable confession? *My
God, my God, why have you forsaken me?* Psalm 22, verse 1.

Jesus is not the first to pray the question of God's seeming
abandonment. He prays out of his tradition by offering the
psalmist's lament. *Lament.* Of all the words and prayers the
church has inherited from our Judaic roots, those of lament
have been grossly overlooked. We read them and feel uncomfortable, believing it impolite to address God in such terms.

How long? Why have you forsaken me? Or we want to rush past the lament and get to the celebration. Some commentators quickly point to Psalm 22's confident ending as evidence that Jesus' prayer of forsakenness is actually a veiled cry of praise for deliverance. Jesus' quoting the opening line of this psalm may invite us to consider the whole of its message. But remember: Jesus does not quote Psalm 22 from verse 22 on (where praise and deliverance come to the forefront) to make us think about this psalm. Jesus prays verse 1. Only in confronting the awe-ful reality of abandonment and forsakenness do the other themes of this psalm come into full, gracious, and mysterious view.

Just as Jesus is not the first to pray the question of God's seeming abandonment, he is not the last. His prayer encourages us to pray honestly to God. We cannot deceive God in prayer or in living. Forming our prayers so as not to offend God by covering over deep anxieties or disturbing emotions is an exercise in vanity. Jesus' experience of forsakenness on the cross became his prayer. We can argue until doomsday whether in fact God had abandoned Jesus or fled from the scene or in any other way disassociated God's self from the Beloved. But Jesus' prayer makes no sense had he not been feeling forsaken. Jesus prayed out of his experience: "My God, my God . . . " Jesus does not let go of God, even in lament. He prays honest to God.

So Jesus' prayer teaches us to pray—in all honesty, not only when God seems distant and removed but when it comes to our doubts or fears or alienation in relationships. Our prayers simply yet profoundly seek to reveal the truth of ourselves and our experiences to God that we might open the reality of our lives to the grace of God.

Honestly.

*My God, my God, what a gift to call upon you when I feel you close
or sense you far away, in my strength or in my weakness, when all is
crystal clear or when nothing makes sense. Amen.*

Spiritual Exercise

Read Matthew 27:46. What has ever brought you close to, or
resulted in, your raising similar words of lament in prayer?
Why? In your journal, reflect on a particular time in your life
when you may have found it difficult to be honest in your
prayers. What created the difficulties? In what ways were those
difficulties connected to your relationship with or beliefs about
God? Identify one particular issue or struggle in your current
experience that might benefit from greater candor in prayer.
Pray about that matter now. Be frank as you bring that concern before God. Be willing to listen in new ways.

Day 4

A Prayer Not Offered

"Save yourself . . . !
"Let the Messiah, the King of Israel,
come down from the cross now,
so that we may see and believe."
—Mark 15:30, 32

IN THE MID-TWENTIETH century, the psychologist Abraham Maslow developed a theory of human motivation that has come to be known as the "hierarchy of needs." Maslow identified six levels of needs or motivations that drive human activity, ranging from primary needs for physical survival and security to more advanced needs for self-fulfillment and understanding. One of the fundamental arguments underlying this hierarchy is that primary needs require satisfaction before an individual will venture toward more abstract motivations for behavior. Self-actualization, the highest motivation, presumes that the needs for survival have been met.

Two millennia before Maslow, people already understood that survival was the bottom line. "Save yourself" witnesses in its own mocking way to the presumption that preserving our own skin is always and everywhere our first priority and driving motivation. Dead messiahs attract no followers. But when we listen to the crowd gathered beneath the cross tossing about words such as those quoted above, we should not mistake their comments as mere taunts spewed in extraordinarily bad taste. Those in the crowd may be threatened by what they see and perhaps even more by what they do *not* hear.

"Holy God, remove these nails, redeem my life from those who would take it, and show them your victory in my triumph." That is the prayer the tormentors seek of Jesus. Why? If nothing happens, they find themselves and their accusations vindicated. If something happens, then they still have time to change their minds, at least for the time being or until the next testing of the primary need to survive comes.

But as has been the case with the whole of his life, Jesus lives and prays out of a different hierarchy of motivations. Survival, "save me," does not summarize the purpose of incarnation. Numerous times before, Jesus defied the expectations of the crowd, not to mention the presumptions of religiosity obsessed with institution. When people sought to make him king, Jesus fled into the hills. When religious authorities honored rules over people, Jesus healed on the sabbath and saved a woman caught in adultery. When Peter sought to turn him from a way marked by suffering and dying, Jesus rebuked the disciple and declared the taking up of the cross to be the way to life.

Save yourself, . . . *come down from the cross.* The temptation of these words is nothing new in Jesus' life or our lives. To live as if everything comes down to insuring our survival no matter the cost, to trust God so long as God keeps us out of harm's way, is to be human. "Save me" is the prayer Jesus leaves unuttered on the cross.

Does that mean our prayers must always and everywhere give no account to personal deliverance? No. "Save me" goes unspoken on the cross, because it has already been addressed in the garden. "If you are willing" began that prayer, and Jesus poured out his heart about the passing of this particular cup. The prayer Jesus does not offer on the cross reminds us of our calling to live in Christ and not according to the presumptions of the world, in which life must be preserved at all costs, personally and institutionally. We follow One whose highest motivation is not survival or even longevity but the fullness of a life of faithfulness.

Save yourself, . . . come down from the cross All sorts of invitations beckon us "down" from the vocation that is ours in Christ Jesus. Faithfulness resists the prayer and the life whose purpose is ultimately self-serving. On the cross, we have heard the witness of silence in the prayer Jesus did not offer. Thanks be to God we do not live merely to survive!

In you, O God, is my life. Grant me the freedom to live in the truth of that gift, the courage to live out the call of that gift, the grace to live toward the hope of that gift. Amen.

Spiritual Exercise

Imagine yourself standing in the crowd before the cross. You hear the taunts of onlookers who say, "Save yourself, and come down" to Jesus. What would you say to Christ on the cross? to those who taunt? What questions would rise up within you? Write these thoughts in your journal. Reflect on the connection between your questions and some current experience in your life or community where the motivation of survival may overwhelm other needs or opportunities. Pray about the motivations that drive you in your church involvements, in your family and friendships, in your personal life.

Day 5

NEED AND HUMANITY

"I am thirsty."
—John 19:28

YOU SIT IN the waiting room. Your child has been in an accident. The nurses have taken him for a CT scan and MRI. You wait, wonder, pray. Prayers tend to be neither elegant nor eloquent in those situations. Simple words and phrases come to mind and heart: *whole, safe, heal, please.*

A similar focus on what is simple and pressing may come when trauma strikes. It may not be central to the crisis but rather a telling sign of human need. I once transported in the ambulance a man from our community who had suffered what appeared to be a serious head injury. Placed on a spine board to immobilize him, he regained consciousness now and again during the trip and complained about his back. At the hospital, in the process of moving him for X-rays, someone found that a stone from the quarry where he worked had lodged between his back and the spine board. With all the other injury and trauma the man suffered, that small stone had become the focus of his discomfort during his ride to the hospital. *I am hurting.*

Iron nails pierced palms and feet. Breathing became more labored as lungs filled with liquid that would eventually drown the victim of crucifixion. Exposure to the elements alternately brought on chills and fever. Yet, with all of these things weighing (literally) upon him, Jesus' only expression of physical need from the cross is this: *I am thirsty.*

"I am thirsty." In only one other place in John's Gospel

does Jesus give evidence of thirst and that came when he asked for a drink of water from a Samaritan woman at Jacob's well. In the conversation that followed, Jesus identified himself as the source of living water that brings eternal life. Cynics at the cross might wonder why Jesus does not avail himself of living water now. The cross, however, is not about parlor tricks. It is about suffering, dying, thirsting—and praying.

I am thirsty. Sometimes prayer comes down to basics. *I am...*, with little more than a word or phrase following, can express to God all we are in that moment. "I am hurting ... I am grateful ... I am helpless ... I am yours." For Jesus, this brief phrase *I am thirsty* expresses his most pressing need to God and to anyone who might act in the name of decency to slake that thirst. In the other Gospels, the offering of sour wine (vinegar) to Jesus seems more an act of taunting. John's Gospel, however, treats the scene more respectfully, as if quenching the thirst of a dying man were the one humane act available to an onlooker.

I am thirsty: very human words, very human prayer. To follow Jesus' prayer path in this instance reminds us that we do not leave our humanity behind when we approach God in prayer. As God fashioned us human, so we fashion our prayers, crying out for the meeting of our basic human needs and those of others. We pronounce how it is with us before the One who hears and who, in Jesus, knows how it truly is with us.

I am thirsty. Who you are at any given moment in your life becomes the stuff from which prayers arise. Out of your need, joy, despair, and hope you may pray, as Jesus prayed, who you are. In so praying, you open yourself to God and to the way God may touch you through the gift of another.

I am . . . pray that prayer today. Bare yourself, your mind, your heart, and your relationships to God. In offering the truth of who you are, be open to the grace of discovering even more deeply whose you are.

Sometimes, O God, it is not easy to admit our humanity or our needs to you, not to mention to ourselves. Help us pray the simple truth of our lives, in hope of the simple gift of your grace. Amen.

Spiritual Exercise

In your journal, write "I am ... " at the top of a page. Beneath it, write words or simple phrases that reveal something of your needs, feelings, and hopes at this moment in your life. Take time to pray over each of those entries. Consider how they speak of your relationship with God and others. After you have prayed, think of one thing you can do, for as many of those entries as possible, that gives expression to your trust in God and to your sense of God's leading in that place in your life. Make a note to come back to this page in the journal in a week to see what may have changed or evolved.

Day 6

FINISHED OR FINISHED?

"It is finished."
—John 19:30

YOU HAVE WORKED on a plan, a dream, a relationship for months, maybe years. You have poured yourself into it, expending hard work, energy, resources, love. But a key thread begins to unravel. An unforeseen obstacle arises; events take a turn for the worse; love is not returned. You helplessly watch as it all disintegrates. You cannot avoid saying in resignation and defeat: "It is finished."

You have worked on a plan, a dream, or a relationship for months, maybe years. You have poured yourself into it, expending hard work, energy, resources, love. Obstacles disappear; all falls into place; love multiplies. You gratefully watch as it comes to completion. You cannot avoid saying in fulfillment and joy: "It is finished."

Opposite ends described by the same turn of phrase *It is finished.* What does it mean?

Beneath the cross, those who taunt and mock see their judgment justified in the ebbing of Jesus' life. No last-minute deliverance, no saving sign from heaven. The blasphemer hangs and bleeds and breathes ever heavier. When they hear Jesus speak these words they probably nod their heads in agreement. Yes, it is—yes, you are—finished.

Upon the cross, the crucified one nears his last breath. Three years of ministry pass by in mind's eye. Mother and friend keep constant vigil. Looking back, looking around, looking ahead,

Jesus cannot help but offer a prayer of completion and accomplishment: "It is finished." The same event described by the same turn of phrase but with totally opposite meanings.

It is finished. We can understand Jesus' prayer in two dramatically different ways. The one we choose becomes a confessional statement of sorts, revealing our view of what occurs on the cross. Just the same, how (and when) you pray "it is finished" reflects the faith you bring, the God you discern, and the hope you carry in this life.

It is finished. Jesus' prayer "hands over" his work to God. The purposes of God's sending the Beloved have been fulfilled. The work is done. Now comes the time to let go, to entrust. Some things, even for Jesus, go beyond his calling and responsibility.

In Jesus' prayer, we catch a glimpse of what comes hard for us: letting go, entrusting. When we complete some work or task or relationship, we want to hold on. We want things to stay as they are or at least as we have known them to be. Jesus knows when he has reached the limits of his ministry, and he prays with confidence, *It is finished.* Jesus affirms his own work and opens the door to the remarkable work of God in Easter and to the empowering work of the Spirit on Pentecost.

Completion brings closure, and closure can bring new beginnings. Traveling the prayer paths of Jesus, *It is finished* imposes two disciplines upon us. First, we remain steadfast in our work and ministry until it is done. Jesus did not pray these words when he got tired of the job midway through or mad at followers who never seemed to grasp the mission. This prayer holds true in our lives when we hold to the course. In an ultimate sense, the prayer awaits our final breath. But before we reach that point, times will come when we need to recognize completion of our work in order to move on. Second, this prayer seeks a readiness to acknowledge what is completed, accept it, and move on. Remember, what was "finished" on the cross was *not* the entire work of God but of Jesus' earthly ministry. Likewise, what we "finish" may continue after us, taken up by other hands in different ways.

And that is good. No one of us can do the labor required to bring the sovereign realm of God upon earth. God never intended that for us, not even for Jesus. God seeks those who keep faith in the tasks and times given, persons and communities whose fulfillment comes in finishing the parts entrusted to us, as we then entrust them to God.

It is finished. May we pray those words with gratitude for opportunities fulfilled, with trust for other hands perfecting our work, and with hope that God will bring all to completion.

Alpha and Omega, you who hold all our beginnings and endings: Grant me the strength to complete what you give me to do, the peace to let go what is no longer mine to carry, and the wisdom to know the difference. Amen.

Spiritual Exercise

In your journal, prayerfully reflect on these three questions:

(1) What do I truly need to finish or complete in my faith journey?

(2) What have I finished that I need to let go of in my life?

(3) Where do I see God calling me to new work or service?

Consider how your responses to these three questions intertwine in ways that complement or contradict one another. Pray God's spirit to guide you in the coming days as you seek to move these reflections from "paper" into life.

Day 7

THE HANDS OF GOD

"Father, into your hands I commend my spirit."
—Luke 23:46

ANDS. WITH THEM, we touch the world around us.
We hold hands as an act of love. We take a child's
hand in ours and lead him or her on the way. We
stroke the hand of a dying one to convey our presence. We fold
hands in prayer. To have something or someone entrusted into
our hands conveys responsibility.

In the Passion narrative, human hands do not act kindly or
justly toward Jesus. Following his arrest, Jesus' examiners use
hands to strike him in the face. The guards take whip in hand to
flog him. Pilate washes his hands to abdicate responsibility. Nails
driven through Jesus' own hands impale him on crossed timbers.

We could understand if Jesus wanted nothing to do with
hands in his final moments, given the pain and betrayal that
have flowed from hands ever since he had been handed over.
Yet Jesus' final words of prayer take the form of enfolding
hands: "Father, into your hands I commend my spirit."

In that act of trust, Jesus hints that God's work is far from
over. While Good Friday may mark the last of Jesus' acts in his
earthly life, Jesus' prayer of commendation leaves the door
open for God's hands to make what they will of Jesus' spirit.
Even when Jesus' hands fall limp in death and find themselves
bound by linen grave cloths, God's hands remain free: free to
craft a new act of creation, free to summon life out of death as
it had once been summoned out of the formless void. Radical

hope, not resignation, forms the essence of Jesus' final prayer that entrusts not merely the past and present but the future into God's hands.

God's hands. Our prayers often draw from the wells of our tradition. Jesus' final prayer breathes almost verbatim a commendation rendered in a psalm of deliverance (31:5). Both psalmist and Jesus entrust life and spirit into the hands of God. And why not? Creation bears the life-giving touch of God's fingers (Psalm 8:3). God's inscribing Zion "on the palm of my hands" (Isaiah 49:16) assured that God's own would not be forgotten. The hands of God cradle our beginnings; the hands of God enfold our hope.

Father, into your hands I commend my spirit. When we follow the prayer paths of Jesus, we recognize life's source and destiny in the hands of God. We do not pray from a spirit of desperation, grasping for a hope or truth never experienced. We have known the touch of God's hands all along. Those cupped hands lifted the waters of the Spirit, pouring them over us freely in baptism. Those hands have taken hold of ours, with and without our awareness, to lead, to love, to chide, to nurture. In whatever way life unfolds for us, those hands will beckon us forward when we might otherwise balk, lift us up when we may fall, stroke us when we need assurance and comfort. And in our final words and prayers, those hands will be there to receive us.

In Luke's Gospel Jesus utters this final prayer in a *loud* voice. This prayer to God cannot help but be heard by friend and foe gathered beneath the cross, by you and me. There is no secret, no denying: Jesus entrusts himself to God. His shout begets the question, And what of us? To whom do we entrust ourselves, not only at the moment of death but all along the way? Jesus' final prayer uttered on Calvary is but a culmination of prayer, life, and ministry that has always been in the hands of God.

Father, into your hands I commend my spirit. You need not put these words on hold until your dying breath. Traveling the prayer paths of Jesus invites you to begin each day entrusting yourself wholly into God's hands.

So may you live . . . in God's hands.

Grace me, O God, to feel your hands beneath me, to experience the creative touch of your fingers upon me, to reach with your outstretched hand to others in compassion. In Jesus Christ. Amen.

Spiritual Exercise

Look closely at your hands. Recall how it felt when they touched the hand of a friend or loved one this week. Imagine yourself being held in the hands of God. Spend a few moments allowing that image to fill your mind and spirit. What would those hands feel like upon you? What do you most need from those hands at this time in your life? Pray Luke 23:46, entrusting your life into the hands of God. Pray for those with special needs known to you, and pray God's hands to enfold them. Visualize touching the hands of God, and thank God for the grace of God's hands holding you.

Epilogue

PRAYER AS BLESSING AND RECOGNITION

When [Jesus] was at the table with them,
he took bread, blessed and broke it, and gave it to them.
Then their eyes were opened, and they recognized him. . . .

Then [Jesus] led them out as far as Bethany, and,
lifting up his hands, he blessed them.
While he was blessing them,
he withdrew from them and was carried up into heaven.

And [the disciples] were continually in the temple blessing God.

—Luke 24:30-31, 50-51, 53

*T*HE THREAD of blessing stitches together the ending of Luke's Gospel. Blessing extends from bread to disciples to God. With blessing comes recognition of a risen Lord, a new life, and a God worthy of praise. At its heart, prayer involves both blessing and recognition. The blessing of food invites recognition of Provider. The blessing of persons invokes recognition of relationship. The blessing of God elicits recognition of life's source and goal and gracing of its days.

This volume has explored the prayers of Jesus, their settings and words, as a means of forming our prayers in Christ's example. Jesus did not "teach us to pray" in only one instance. Throughout his life and ministry, even in the hour of his dying, Jesus modeled a life of prayer. Now in Luke's record of Jesus' resurrection appearances, we encounter Jesus at prayer once more.

On the roadside walk to Emmaus, words and teachings may have burned within those two disciples accompanied by one who remains as a stranger to them. Recognition does not come until hands lift bread and voice speaks a prayer of blessing. Prayer invites and enables recognition. Traveling the prayer paths of Jesus helps us recognize that we stand not only on holy ground but in holy presence. We recognize the One in whose name we pray moving in Spirit in our midst, transforming the common elements of life into opportunities for sacred encounter.

At the hillside town of Bethany, Jesus' blessing falls upon disciples. Traveling the prayer paths of Jesus bids us share our own prayerful blessings with those we count as companions on this journey. Jesus' departure from Bethany also falls upon disciples in their vocation to be the body of Christ on earth. Often we speak of vocation in terms of service, ministry, and mission as we embody the work Christ would do through us. But that vocation also bids us to pray as Jesus prayed, to offer blessing not only to our companions but to all those graced to be God's children. In Christ, we recognize our prayers may stretch as far as God's love.

And in the temple of Jerusalem, the disciples' blessings fall anew upon God. Following Jesus' prayer path returns us in thanksgiving and gratitude to the One to whom Jesus' prayers ascended and to whom Jesus' life pointed. Our prayers are not empty words spoken into an uncaring void. God blesses us with the gift of prayer, and our blessings and prayers return to God in grateful response. For we recognize in Christ the God who graces us with the access of prayer.

May you find such grace to travel the prayer paths of Jesus.
Blessings on the journey!

LEADER'S GUIDE

TO

TRAVELING
THE
PRAYER PATHS
OF JESUS

∾

USING THIS GUIDE

SETTING THE CONTEXT

Traveling the Prayer Paths of Jesus leads readers through the prayers of Jesus recorded in the Gospels and invites them to enter the prayer as a way of transforming their own practices of prayer. The dual focus on the settings of prayer as well as on the actual prayers of Jesus acknowledges that our spiritual formation in the Christian tradition always returns us to Christ. His is the name we bear, and in whose name we pray, even as it is in Jesus' example we may continue to learn the art and gift of prayer.

Traveling the Prayer Paths of Jesus is organized in a six-week series of daily scripture readings. Each daily reading concludes with a prayer and an exercise involving a discipline of spiritual formation. Those exercises are key for integrating daily scripture readings into daily practice of prayer. The session guides that follow will also incorporate some exercises. Within each week, the first scripture reading will introduce the prayers (or prayer settings) encountered in that week's text. For further information on the book's outline and themes, please read the foreword to *Traveling the Prayer Paths of Jesus*.

In prestudy publicity and in reminders at each session, invite participants to bring their journals and copies of *Traveling the Prayer Paths of Jesus* to each session. While participants may not need Bibles at every session, they may wish to bring them for reference or personal use.

TIMES AND SEASONS

Traveling the Prayer Paths of Jesus and this leader's guide have been written with a six-week unit in mind. The chapters are intentionally divided according to numbers of days, rather than to specific days of the week, so that the group may feel free to choose any day as its meeting day. In promoting the book, be sure to encourage participants to read the first chapter, one day at a time, during the week before your first meeting so everyone has a common starting point in the study.

While the book and guide may be used at any time of the year, additional Lenten Emphasis ideas are incorporated into each section of the session guides for those who want to use the book during Lent.

SESSION COMPONENTS

Each session in this guide contains the following components:

- Preparation
- Opening
- Insights
- Explorations
- Closing

Preparation includes these elements: "Preparing to Lead," suggestions for the leader in preparing to lead the session; "Preparing the Room and Materials," an overview of preparation options for the meeting area, including needed materials; and "Preparing to Focus," a summary statement of the session's goals.

The Opening includes suggestions for gathering and welcoming, introducing the theme, a liturgical act and prayer, and a suggested song.

The Insights component provides activities, discussions, and exercises that draw upon the participants' reading and engagement in the spiritual exercises over the past week. Each of those suggestions are followed by ideas for connecting them to Lent.

The Explorations component invites participants into deeper

reflection, engagement in prayer, and/or experiences of the week's theme. Again, directions for use of each of these suggestions in Lent are provided.

The Closing consists of opportunities to summarize and respond to the session, closing acts of worship and/or prayer, and use of the song suggested at the beginning of the session.

The sessions in this guide have been written for use in time periods ranging from forty-five minutes to about one hour. You may adapt them to meet your particular needs.

APPENDIX

The appendix at the end of this guide lists the sources of songs suggested in the guide for use in each session. Four of the songs can be found in hymnals or songbooks that are readily accessible to most churches. I provide the words to another song since no copyright exists. Upper Room Books grants one-time rights to use the words (written by me) of that song in connection with this study. For use in another setting, please contact Upper Room Books.

LEADER AS PARTICIPANT—AND ADAPTER

The format of *Traveling the Prayer Paths of Jesus* promotes a discipline of daily reading, reflection, and spiritual formation. Encourage participants to maintain that daily vigil. It may be possible to cram readings into one or two days—but the exercises of spiritual formation suggested for each day will thrive best when given focus one day at a time.

Give yourself that same opportunity and responsibility. With sessions to prepare, you may find yourself looking ahead to the week's later readings and exercises to gain perspective on the flow and to make plans for the session. Remember, however, that this book and the sessions are as much for your benefit as for the participants'. Allow yourself the grace each day of attending to these stories, their settings and prayers, and of reflecting upon them and engaging in the spiritual exercises. Your best preparation for this study is in sharing the same process of discovery and discipline that you encourage in the participants.

As you come to activities, conversations, or exercises in this guide that might benefit from modification or adjustment, do not feel constrained to lead each and every time as the guide suggests. Allow the suggestions in the guide to provide a structure that frees you to devote time to your own engagement with its words and prayers and exercises.

Enjoy this experience of leading and participating. Hear, as you guide others to hear, Jesus' prayers in new ways. Let these prayers and their settings form your prayer life as you engage in this experience of spiritual formation. God be with you!

SESSION PLAN
FOR
WEEK ONE

Out of Solitude

❧

PREPARATION

Preparing to Lead

Read chapter 1 of *Traveling the Prayer Paths of Jesus* (one reading each day), and do each of the daily spiritual exercises. As suggested in the book's foreword, keep a journal of your reflections generated by the readings and exercises. Maintain a discipline of daily prayer that grows out of the readings and exercises. Review this guide early in the week to allow adequate time for preparation of the session's activities. Pray for each participant you expect to attend and for those who may come unexpectedly, and pray for God's leading in your service as group leader.

Preparing the Room and Materials

Set chairs in a circle around a table to be used for the worship center or in a semicircle facing the worship center (depending on the number of persons in the group). Place a candle on the table along with matches or a lighter. If you have access to a picture or sculpture of hands folded in prayer or to some other visual representation of prayer, place it on the worship center table. Display around the room photographs or paintings of mountains, desert scenes, and/or other natural settings of solitude if you have such resources available.

For this session's Explorations activity, make sure other areas of the church are accessible for prayer in solitude (accessibility will include having heat and lights on in those areas). If your church building has multiple activities planned during the time of your group's session, secure permission to reserve areas for prayer other than your meeting room.

Preparing to Focus

To deepen participants' appreciation for solitude in the life of prayer, as revealed in the prayers of Jesus.

OPENING

➤ Greet participants by name as they enter. Arrange for persons to introduce themselves.

➤ Welcome the gathered participants to this series of group experiences based on *Traveling the Prayer Paths of Jesus*. Call attention to the first paragraph in the book's foreword on learning, as the first disciples sought to do, the art of prayer from Jesus. Underscore that this and future sessions will focus on spiritual formation through the discipline of prayer modeled on Jesus' examples. Impress upon the participants that keeping up with both the daily readings and the spiritual exercises will be critical to the usefulness of the sessions in helping them experience that spiritual formation.

> *Lenten Emphasis*: Explain that Lent has traditionally been a time for persons in the church to engage in disciplines of spiritual formation and transformation. Affirm the hope that this series of sessions will provide such an opportunity to grow as disciples through prayer.

➤ Light the candle on the worship center table. Explain that the candle will be lit at the beginning of each session to symbolize the presence of Christ, the One from whom we would learn to pray.

➤ Offer a brief invocation or prayer inviting God's spirit to touch the group through the words, actions, and silences of this session, to learn from Jesus' prayers in solitude.

> *Lenten Emphasis:* Include in the prayer a thought about the journey the church makes in the season of Lent from Ash Wednesday through the events of Passion Week, culminating in Easter. Pray that the journey this year will strengthen discipleship by encouraging a more vital prayer life.

➤ Lead the group in singing the first two verses of "Come and Find the Quiet Center." (See appendix.) If the tune is unfamiliar, the words can also be sung to the tunes of "Joyful, Joyful, We Adore Thee" or "Glorious Things of Thee Are Spoken." Encourage the participants to reflect on the words of the song words and their connection to this session's focus on Jesus' prayers offered in places and times of solitude.

INSIGHTS

➤ Invite each person to identify one fresh insight he or she gained from this week's readings and/or exercises on prayer and solitude. If participants have kept journals, they may wish to refer to them for their response.

➤ Discuss how their insights might influence and shape their practices of prayer as individuals and how the church community might encourage such renewal. Wait on this discussion until everyone has had an opportunity to share (if persons choose not to speak, honor their silence).

Lenten Emphasis: Reflect on how your church's Lenten programs and worship might lend themselves to and support this renewal.

➤ Encourage persons to make a commitment to incorporate at least one of the shared insights into their discipline of prayer and solitude.

Lenten Emphasis: A traditional custom of Lent has persons "give up" a habit or luxury for the duration of the Lenten season. Invite participants to redirect this custom by "taking on" a new practice of discipleship through a commitment to one of the shared insights into prayer and solitude.

EXPLORATIONS

➤ Affirm the placement of Jesus' prayers in settings of solitude by all the week's scripture readings. Point out that participants' readings and exercises this week likely took place in some degree of solitude. Explain that the session will continue now with an experience of solitary prayer. Just as the Gospels record no words from these prayers of Jesus in solitude, no specific assignment or "agenda" will be given as to what participants may pray for or about in this time. Direct individuals to open and available areas of the church building where they can be alone in prayer. Remind them that prayer is not always about talking to God—but listening as well.

Lenten Emphasis: Encourage individuals to keep in the back of their minds and hearts the season and movement of Lent as they enter this time of prayerful solitude.

➤ Carry out the "dispersal" of participants to various locations. Give them an idea of how and when you will gather them together (the time you allot will depend on the session length: provide a minimum of ten minutes, though fifteen or twenty minutes would be better).

➤ Regather the group members in the meeting room. Invite them to offer one-phrase or simple-sentence responses to their prayer experience.

Lenten Emphasis: Invite participants to share one hope each has for the group's spiritual formation during the Lenten season.

CLOSING

➤ Observe a time of silent prayer together. Direct participants' attention to the light of the candle, to the experience of Christ's presence in this time together.

Lenten Emphasis: Close the silent prayer by calling the group to remember that the light leading us through Lent is Jesus' journey toward Jerusalem, that the prayers he offers along the way illumine our practice of prayer as his disciples.

➤ Sing the first and last verses of "Come and Find the Quiet Center."

➤ Remind participants to read chapter 2, one section each day, and to do the related spiritual exercises. Encourage those who have not kept a journal to try to do so for this week.

SESSION PLAN
FOR
WEEK TWO

By the Roadside

~

PREPARATION

Preparing to Lead

Read chapter 2 of *Traveling the Prayer Paths of Jesus* (one section each day), and do each of the daily spiritual exercises. Continue journaling as you reflect on the readings and exercises. Assess your experience of the first session: what worked well, what did not, what questions might be brought to this week's session by you or by the participants. Make notes of these concerns. Keep them in mind, heart, and prayer as you review the guide to this session early in the week. Use your learnings and experiences from last week to plan the upcoming session. Pray for the participants as you prepare, and seek God's direction in your leadership of the group.

Preparing the Room and Materials

Set chairs around a table to be used for the worship center or in a semicircle facing the worship center. Place a candle on the table, along with matches or a lighter. Display photographs, posters, and/or other images of roadside scenes. Try to depict a diversity of settings and persons one might encounter on the roads of your community and nearby rural and urban areas.

Preparing to Focus

To open participants to the practice of prayer "by the road-side"—for the expected and unexpected opportunities and persons and situations one encounters in daily life.

OPENING

➤ Greet participants by name as they enter. If any were not present at the previous session, take time to introduce them as needed. If time permits before the session begins, brief new participants on this series and on some of the group's experiences and activities from last week's session.

➤ Invite participants to view the display of scenes and persons you have assembled, without yet explaining its connection to this session. Ask individuals to comment on what they see in the pictures and on what the pictures might share in common. Draw the conversation to an affirmation of these scenes and to the persons within them as ordinary images of life, not unlike those encountered in your community or nearby areas. If you have no display, invite participants to identify what they saw while walking or driving to this gathering. Encourage them to be specific (for example, not simply noting "other people" but their dress, activities, and evidenced feelings). Focus on the ordinary nature of these scenes, which are not unlike the scenes Jesus encountered.

> *Lenten Emphasis*: Recall that the ministry of Jesus takes place in "changing" scenes set in ordinary places of daily life: in markets, on roads, in places of worship, in homes. Following Jesus on the Lenten journey in the biblical stories, as in our own lives, need not take us to exotic locations, only to places where life is commonly

lived. Lent sensitizes us to the presence of the holy in those common places of life.

➤ Light the candle on the worship center table. As you do so, invite participants to pray silently for Christ's presence and leading in this gathering. Encourage prayers for the opening of spirits to those encountered on daily journeys, in ordinary places of living, and in this group.

➤ Lead the group in singing the first two verses of "We Meet You, O Christ." (See appendix.) If the tune is unfamiliar or difficult, the words can also be sung to the tune of "O Worship the King" or "Ye Servants of God." Encourage participants as they sing to keep in mind the faces in the display or faces encountered this day, in whom we meet the Christ among us on the road.

INSIGHTS

➤ Invite participants to offer comments, share experiences, or raise questions stirred by the week's readings and daily exercises.

➤ Ask the group to look over their journaling entries from the past week. Invite willing persons to share what spoke most deeply to them this week.

> *Lenten Emphasis*: Help participants identify ways in which their insights and journal entries relate to their Lenten experiences or hopes. In particular, encourage them to share their observations about the effect of these exercises and disciplines on their individual observance of Lent. Ask the group, **How has your experience of the journey toward Jerusalem been shaped this week?**

EXPLORATIONS

➤ Ask the participants to form pairs. Call attention to the emphasis in the "Spiritual Exercise" for Day 1 on routine in life and prayer. Invite the partners to reflect with each other on ways in which their routine of prayer and/or living was influenced by practicing this discipline. Be prepared, as a way of helping partners start their conversations, to speak to this subject from your own experience. At the end of this reflection time, invite the partners to pray for each other.

> *Lenten Emphasis*: Ask the partners to identify routines associated with Lent in the church and in their own experience. Encourage them to explore those routines together in light of the spiritual exercise for Day 1. Ask them to consider what purposes and goals those routines may (or may not) serve or ignore.

➤ Invite all the group members to close their eyes, breathe deeply, and relax as they listen and participate in this narrative of Jesus' public ministry from Matthew (9:35-36). Allow time for reflection wherever there is a break (. . .) between lines.

> **"Then Jesus went about all the cities and villages . . ."** (*Imagine Jesus walking down the street that passes by your church, not in the dress of a first-century Israelite but a twenty-first-century resident of your neighborhood.*) . . . (*The street on which Jesus walks is unusually busy today. Perhaps it is a holiday or some other occasion when people are out and about.*) . . . **"When he saw the crowds, he had compassion for them, because they were harassed and helpless . . ."** (*What do the people in your neighborhood look and act like when they feel harassed and helpless? What do you look and act like in such times?*) . . . (*Imagine Jesus walking up to you. What would*

he do for you, now, that would reveal compassion? . . . What would he do for people you see on the street all the time? . . . What would Jesus have you do for them?) . . .

Ask everyone to open his or her eyes and take several deep breaths. Invite responses to this experience. Ask participants what part of the experience remains with them. Invite them to share what they are being invited to do, offer, or receive.

Lenten Emphasis: Say to the group, **Lent offers us an opportunity to reflect on Jesus' response to human need with grace and compassion and prayer and to accept the challenge to discipline our lives to do as he did.** Invite individuals to reflect on ways in which this guided imagery experience can speak to their encounters with others and with Christ during the Lenten season.

CLOSING

➤ Invite the participants to identify one gift or insight they will take with them from this gathering. When all who want to have shared, encourage them to reflect silently on the power of that gift or insight to influence their prayerful interactions with the individuals and needs they encounter along their faith journey. Invite them to offer sentence prayers that invoke God's help and leading as they seek to grow in prayer and service on their journey.

Lenten Emphasis: Before beginning the sentence prayers, ask the participants to recall the disciples who first followed Jesus. Remind them that although Jerusalem and Passion Week stood at their journey's close, the path wound its way through small villages and ordinary folk and common needs. Jesus' practice of prayer in those contexts invites our own prayer discipline as we wind our way through ordinary places of living.

➤ Sing the first and second verses of "We Meet You, O Christ."

➤ Remind participants to read chapter 3, one reading each day, and to do the related spiritual exercises. Continue to encourage the keeping of the journal. Have participants bring Bibles with them to the next session.

SESSION PLAN
FOR
WEEK THREE

On the Mountainside

~

PREPARATION

Preparing to Lead

Read chapter 3 of *Traveling the Prayer Paths of Jesus* (one section each day), and do each of the daily spiritual exercises. Continue journaling as you reflect on the readings and exercises. Assess your experiences of the initial sessions: what worked well, what did not, what questions might be brought to this week's session by you or by the participants. Make notes of these concerns. Keep them in mind and heart and prayer as you review this session guide early in the week. Use learnings and experiences from prior weeks to plan the upcoming session. Pray for the participants as you prepare, and seek God's direction in your leadership of the group.

Preparing the Room and Materials

Create a worship center by using a table covered with a plain cloth. On the table, place a Bible open to Matthew 6. Find and display copies of the Lord's Prayer, different versions and perhaps even different languages. Your pastor and/or church library might be able to provide these resources. If your Christian education or spiritual formation department has a collection of artwork, find pictures of Jesus teaching the crowds and/or of persons leading prayer or joining another person in prayer.

Display these images around or above the worship center. In the middle of the worship center table, place a candle, along with matches or a lighter. Have paper and pencils available for participants' use.

Preparing to Focus

To explore and offer anew the words Jesus taught his disciples long ago, and still today, to pray.

OPENING

➤ Greet participants by name as they enter. If any were not present at the previous sessions, take time to introduce them.

➤ Ask the participants to form groups of three or four. Ask the members of each group to share briefly an early memory of learning to pray and of the person(s) who taught them.

> *Lenten Emphasis:* Invite participants to reflect briefly on their Lenten journey thus far and on the focus of these sessions on forming our prayers in the light of Jesus' own practices and the settings of his prayers.

➤ Light the candle on the worship center table, and invite participants to pray silently and gratefully for early experiences of learning to pray and for Christ's presence and leading as they further that formation in prayer through the prayer Jesus taught. At the end of the silent prayer time, ask the group to unite in the Lord's Prayer.

➤ Sing or pray the verse of "Prayer Is the Soul's Sincere Desire" printed in the appendix. The words may be sung to the tune of "Amazing Grace" or "O for a Thousand Tongues to Sing." Encourage participants to offer the song as a prayer, invoking Christ's presence to guide anew the experience of the Lord's Prayer in this session.

INSIGHTS

➤ Invite participants to offer comments, share experiences, or raise questions stirred by this week's readings and daily exercises. Encourage them to refresh their memories by reviewing notes or entries in their journals. Allow them to spend time in conversation about the past week as needed.

➤ Direct participants to the "Spiritual Exercise" following the text for Day 1 of this week in *Traveling the Prayer Paths of Jesus*. Invite them to share brief recollections generated by the two opening questions. Move the conversation to the associations, memories, and voices that have influenced the participants' praying and/or valuing of the Lord's Prayer.

> *Lenten Emphasis*: Invite participants to reflect on ways in which the Lord's Prayer fits with the season and mood of Lent. Ask them to identify and reflect on any special or intentional ways in which they have experienced the Lord's Prayer during Lent (for example, worship series, study or prayer group emphasis).

➤ Ask each person to write down one insight of personal significance gleaned from any of this week's readings and/or spiritual exercises. Instruct the participants to return to their earlier groups of three or four persons. Invite willing individuals to share with the small group these three things: the petition of the Lord's Prayer that touched them most deeply, the insight they received, and the importance of that insight to them. Some persons may choose not to share. Allow them to do so. Explain that the other members of each group initially will listen, giving no reactions or feedback but a word of thanks for sharing. When all who wish to have spoken, have members engage in conversation within the groups about what has been shared. These conversations should focus on what made an insight personally important to the individual.

Lenten Emphasis: Move the conversations to explore ways in which an insight of personal importance can shape Lent's invitation to follow Christ more closely or deeply.

EXPLORATIONS

➤ Read aloud the opening paragraph of the Day 1 text. Distribute paper and pencils to the participants, and ask them to write down their responses to the two questions at the end of the paragraph. Provide sufficient time for them to carry out this assignment.

➤ Ask the participants to find partners and share their answers. Encourage them to discuss the relationship of necessities and the reasons for them to what we offer God and what we seek from God.

Lenten Emphasis: Explain the Lenten tradition of providing a time and season in which individuals and communities of faith focus on priorities, either by renouncing things of lesser importance or by taking up the cross of discipleship. Ask partners to explore how necessities and/or the reasons for them might be transformed by the priorities of Lent's journey toward the cross.

➤ Read aloud Matthew 6:9-13 while participants follow along in their Bibles. Pause between each petition of the prayer. During those pauses, invite participants to consider why that petition is necessary not simply to the prayer but to his or her own life. Explain that you will read each petition aloud again and that after each one, willing persons are invited to share how that petition speaks of a necessity in their life. Be comfortable with silence if some petitions garner no response. Do not interpret what persons say, but thank them for sharing.

Lenten Emphasis: Invite participants to reflect on how they might use the Lord's Prayer during this season of Lent: in personal devotion, as a daily call to faith, in corporate worship, as a remembrance of their true necessities in life.

CLOSING

➤ Allow participants the opportunity to offer brief comments on what they have gained from this session and to ask any questions that might have been generated.

Lenten Emphasis: Encourage participants to use the Lord's Prayer in at least one new way or with fresh attention in this Lenten season.

➤ Sing the verse of "Prayer Is the Soul's Sincere Desire" whose words are printed in the appendix.

➤ Ask the group to form a circle and join hands. Explain that the session will close with the group's offering of the Lord's Prayer in the following way. You will begin by saying, "Our Father." The person to your right will continue by saying the next one or more petitions of the prayer. The next person to the right will do the same. Praying will continue around the circle until each person has offered at least part of the prayer, which means, depending on the size of the group, the whole prayer may be said several times. Affirm that persons who do not wish to or are unable to speak aloud may simply squeeze the hand of the person to their right, and that individual will continue with the prayer circle. Invite the group to be attentive to the different voices lent to the petitions of the prayer, a reminder that the Lord's Prayer belongs to the whole people of God.

➤ Remind participants to read chapter 4, one section each day, and to do the related spiritual exercises. Continue to encourage the keeping of the journal.

SESSION PLAN
FOR
WEEK FOUR

In the Upper Room

~

PREPARATION

Preparing to Lead

Read chapter 4 of *Traveling the Prayer Paths of Jesus* (one section each day), and do each of the daily spiritual exercises. Continue journaling as you reflect on the readings and exercises. Review any notes you have taken on the first three sessions and recall evaluation comments you may have received from participants. Use these learnings as you review the guide to this session early in the week and begin to make plans for leading the session. Consider what, if any, of the suggestions may need to be adapted. Pray for the participants as you prepare, and seek God's direction in your leadership of this group.

Preparing the Room and Materials

Set chairs around a table to be used for the worship center or in a semicircle facing the worship center. Place a candle on the table, along with matches or a lighter. If the church has a painting of Jesus' face or one depicting him at prayer, display it on or near the worship center. Have enough note cards (3-by-5 or 4-by-6) and pencils so every participant has one of each.

Preparing to Focus

To acknowledge and broaden the participants' community of prayer—persons who pray for them and those for whom they pray—and that they will receive the grace of knowing themselves prayed for by Christ.

OPENING

➤ Greet participants by name as they enter. Offer words of welcome to guests or newcomers, as well as a brief introduction to this study.

➤ Invite participants to pick up a note card and to write their name on one side and on the other side the names of two persons for whom they have prayed this past week. Ask them to set the finished cards either on the worship center table or around the painting of Jesus, if available. In groups of three or four people, invite the group members to share their reasons for praying for the individuals listed on the back of their note cards. Names need not be shared, only something of the person's situation or relationship with the participant that generated prayer. Instruct the groups to listen for similarities and differences in the factors that led to prayer. Reflect on what this conversation reveals about how we come to pray for others.

> *Lenten Emphasis*: Lent is a journey taken by a community of faith. Encourage participants to consider how the names and lives of the persons on the backs of those cards represent a community brought together by prayer in this season of Lent. Ask, **In what ways are the members of that community joined to one another?**

➤ Light the candle on the worship center table, inviting participants to pray silently for Christ's presence and leading in this gathering. Encourage participants to pray silently for those whom they listed on the back of their cards. Close the prayer by acknowledging that in this very moment a community formed by prayer has taken shape in the presence of Christ.

➤ Sing or pray the two verses of "When the Hour of Glory Beckoned" printed in the appendix. The words may be sung to the tune named HYFRYDOL or another written in the meter of 87.87.D (for example, AUSTRIA or HYMN TO JOY). Encourage participants as they sing to visualize the community created in and by Christ's prayers for us.

INSIGHTS

➤ Invite participants to offer comments, share experiences, or raise questions stirred by this week's readings and daily exercises. Encourage them to refresh their memories by reviewing notes or entries in their journals and to spend time in conversation as needed.

➤ Direct participants to the "Spiritual Exercise" for Day 1 in this week's section and in particular to the list in their journals of those they wish to pray for them. Invite participants to describe, without necessarily identifying those persons by name, why they singled them out. Guide participants to focus on relationships, characteristics, personal experiences, and other factors that affected their choices. Turn the question around, and ask participants to reflect silently on who would hold them in such regard as to seek their prayers, and why.

> *Lenten Emphasis*: Lent offers a season of discovery, not only about the way of Jesus but about the way of those called to be disciples. Invite participants to reflect on discoveries discerned in this exercise for Lent's journey in prayer.

EXPLORATIONS

➤ Direct participants' attention to the picture of Christ displayed, if available. If not available, invite them to visualize an image of Jesus at prayer, perhaps in this room, perhaps in your sanctuary.

As participants focus on the picture or visualize, read John 17 as you might pray it. Affirm that these words are Jesus' prayer for disciples of our time, including us. Ask, **If Christ were here now, in this room at this moment in your life, what would he pray? What would be his words for you?** Give participants an opportunity to write a prayer Jesus might offer for each of them. Be sure they understand that the prayer might encourage, comfort, or guide but should address the deepest need in their lives at this moment. Allow sufficient time for them to work on this prayer, perhaps encouraging them to spread out in the meeting room or even beyond.

> *Lenten Emphasis:* To journey with Christ during Lent graces us with the opportunity to listen as Jesus prays for us.

➤ Ask participants to select a trusted partner or pair of partners with whom they would be willing to share the prayer they have written. Again, encourage the partners or trios to find room or space for some privacy. One person begins by reading the prayer he or she wrote. The partner or pair listens and afterward will pray for the one who has shared, based on what has been heard. Each person will close his or her prayer with *I pray for you in the name of Jesus, even as Jesus prays for you now.* This process should be repeated until all have experienced being prayed for.

> *Lenten Emphasis:* Lent risks self-disclosure before God. Yet in that disclosure, we open ourselves not only to

the presence of Christ but to the prayers of Christ for us. Affirm that those with whom we share this journey bear Christ's presence to us and that in their prayers we may hear the prayers of Christ for us.

➤ Gather participants together. Invite responses to what they have experienced and felt while praying for others and while being prayed for in the name of Christ.

CLOSING

➤ Encourage participants to identify one gift or insight they will take with them from this gathering as they continue their journey.

➤ Invite each participant to hold one individual in silent prayer. Use the following or similar words as you guide the participants through this prayer: **The person you pray for may be someone for whom you have a pressing concern or deep gratitude, or someone you simply desire to remember. As you pray, imagine Christ's arms embracing that person and Christ's voice speaking what she or he most needs to hear. As you pray, envision that person and Christ turning to you praying your name and your need.** Allow adequate time for each participant to enter this scene and experience of prayer. Close the exercise with these or similar words: **We pray in Christ's name, even as we hear our name prayed by Christ: by grace, with love. Amen.**

➤ Close by singing or praying the two verses of "When the Hour of Glory Beckoned."

➤ Remind participants to read chapter 5 and to do the related spiritual exercises and journal-keeping. Also invite them to take home the note cards and to use them in their prayers this coming week.

SESSION PLAN
FOR
WEEK FIVE

At the Garden

~

PREPARATION

Preparing to Lead

Read chapter 5 of *Traveling the Prayer Paths of Jesus* (one section each day) and do each of the daily spiritual exercises. Continue with journaling as you reflect on the readings and exercises. Assess your experiences of the initial sessions: what worked well, what did not, what questions might be carried to this next session by you and by the participants. Make notes of these concerns. Keep them in mind and heart and prayer as you review this session guide early in the week. Use the learnings and experiences from prior weeks to plan the upcoming session. Pray for the participants in this preparation, and seek God's direction in your leadership of this group.

Preparing the Room and Materials

Set chairs around a table to be used for the worship center or in a semicircle facing the worship center. Place a candle on the table, along with matches or a lighter, and a cross. Display garden utensils and plants on the worship center and around the room. You might ask several participants to help in providing these. Aromatic plants would be a nice touch, but be sure none of the participants has allergic reactions to such odors.

Preparing to Focus

To experience in Jesus' garden prayers a model for prayerfully and honestly opening one's faith and struggles to God's purposes.

OPENING

➤ Greet participants by name as they enter.

➤ Invite participants to browse through the garden plants and utensils. As they do, encourage them to talk with one another about what they find interesting or challenging or renewing about spending time or working in gardens. Move the conversation to their associations between growth in gardens and growth in faith or spiritual formation.

> *Lenten Emphasis*: Except in the southern hemisphere or very mild climates, the season of Lent (depending on when it falls on the calendar) may be a time when gardens are not in season. Help participants explore connections between the season of Lent and gardens not in season.

➤ Light the candle on the worship center, inviting participants to pray silently for Christ's presence and leading in this gathering. Close the prayer with words and images that connect the opening conversations about gardens and spiritual growth with the garden Jesus entered at Gethsemane, noting that garden's invitation through prayer to grow in Christ.

➤ Sing the first two verses of "Come Away with Me." Encourage participants to visualize as they sing the sort of place the song beckons them to enter, where they may encounter God.

INSIGHTS

➤ Invite participants to offer comments, share experiences, or raise questions stirred by this week's readings and daily exercises. Encourage them to refresh their memories by reviewing notes or entries in their journals. Allow them to spend time in conversation as needed.

➤ Select six participants to read one each of this week's six scriptural readings on Jesus' prayers in Gethsemane (they are listed at the top of the Day 1 text). Instruct those who will be reading to do so slowly and firmly and to leave a space of half a minute between each passage to allow for reflection. Encourage the group to imagine themselves in the garden with Jesus as they listen to these words of or about Jesus' prayers. Carry out the reading. At the end, invite comments on the overall impact of these garden prayers.

> *Lenten Emphasis*: Lent moves us toward the cross, which comes into view perhaps most clearly in Gethsemane. Invite participants to reflect silently on what these prayers say about our discipleship and prayers as we move toward the cross.

➤ Call attention to the Day 1 text's comparison and contrast of mazes and labyrinths, particularly in relation to the experiences of Jesus and disciples in Gethsemane. Request that the participants form groups of three or four. Ask group members to discuss experiences similar to Gethsemane's maze/labyrinth that they have faced in their spiritual journey. Ask them to describe their feelings in those places and to identify the role of prayer (their own or that of others) in moving them through those times.

> *Lenten Emphasis*: "Season" this experience by exploring at the end of the exercise how persons experience

Lent as a labyrinth. Invite participants to consider how they might "pray" their way through the pilgrimage Lent will travel from garden to cross.

EXPLORATIONS

➤ Instruct individuals to find a place where they can work comfortably. Ask them to turn to the Day 4 text and to any journal entries they made based on that text or its accompanying spiritual exercise. Invite participants to pray to themselves several times over the words of Jesus in Luke 22:42: *Not my will but yours be done.* Give these or similar instructions: **As you pray these words, leave spaces of silence for listening and reflection. At this moment, do you struggle about a purpose or "will" of God in your life? What are your inclinations? your hopes? your fears? Each time you pray these words, listen to your own heart for a sense of the heart of God on this matter.** Allow five to ten minutes for such prayer and reflection, then say: **In your journal, write down thoughts that have come to you about your struggle, your options, and where you sense being led or directed. Note also what you find difficult about praying** *not my will but yours.*

> *Lenten Emphasis*: In the liturgy of the church, the stories of Jesus' passion are often presented in ways that would place us there. This activity attempts to provide a way to enter Gethsemane with Jesus, that we might not simply learn more of Jesus' struggle in prayer but see its connection to our lives and prayers.

➤ Ask participants to find a trusted partner. Read Jesus' words from Matthew 26:37-38. Explain that each set of partners will keep the vigil Jesus invited Peter, James, and John to keep with him. That is, one of the partners will share, as he or she feels comfortable, something from the prayer experience above. The "listener" listens, repeats what he or she has heard, and offers a brief prayer for God's guidance. The process should be repeated, so that each partner has an opportunity to share, listen, and pray. Be sure the partners understand that this is not a time for advice or making pronouncements about God's will but a time to offer support.

Lenten Emphasis: Explain that the church journeys through Lent in community with Christ and with one another, sharing struggles as well as faith and deepening the bonds between us and the One who prayed in Gethsemane.

➤ Gather the participants together. Allow opportunity for those who so wish to reflect on their experience in these explorations.

CLOSING

➤ Invite participants to share what they will carry from this "garden" in the way of experiences, questions, and affirmations.

Lenten Emphasis: Ask participants to recall once more that from the garden the Lenten journey moves to the cross. Invite them prayerfully to consider how this session's experiences and prayers will shape their journey to the cross.

➤ Sing the second and fifth verses of "Come Away with Me."

➤ Ask the participants to make a circle and join hands. Call attention one final time to the garden utensils and the cross on the worship center. Say these or similar words: **In Gethsemane Jesus invited his disciples to stay with him as he prayed. So we have been invited to keep this vigil. Luke records that** an angel appeared to Jesus to bring him strength. In our prayers and struggles, we likewise draw strength from God. Let us close with prayers you would offer for the remainder of Lent's journey with Christ. When the prayer draws to a close, offer this commissioning: **Friends, our sojourn and prayers in the garden are done. Golgotha beckons. Let us be going.**

➤ Remind participants to read chapter 6 and daily to keep up with the related spiritual exercises and journal-keeping.

SESSION PLAN
FOR
WEEK SIX

Upon the Cross

∿

PREPARATION

Preparing to Lead

Read chapter 6 of *Traveling the Prayer Paths of Jesus* (one section each day), and do each of the daily spiritual exercises. Continue journaling as you reflect on the readings and exercises. Since this will be the last session, incorporate learnings from previous experiences into your planning. Remember that not all unanswered questions or unfinished discussions can be neatly wrapped up, but anticipate how you might address such issues in this session. Pray for the participants as you prepare, and open yourself to God's leading in this work. Offer thanks for this opportunity to share with the participants in this experience, and consider ways to express that gratitude during the session.

Preparing the Room and Materials

Set a plain white cloth on a table to create a worship center. Place a crucifix (a cross with the figure of Christ on it) on the worship center table. If you do not have a crucifix, use a cross. Place a candle on the table, along with matches or a lighter. If you plan to use a tape recording of the cross prayers in the exploration exercise, prerecord the tape and have a tape player with adequate sound system available. Be sure recordings of instrumental music are available if you plan to use them be-tween the individual cross prayers. If you plan to carry out the Explorations exercise in the sanctuary or another area of the church, make those arrangements ahead of time.

Preparing to Focus

To enter the cross prayers of Jesus as a means of reflecting on the honesty and ultimacy of our own prayers and trust in Christ.

OPENING

➤ Greet participants by name as they enter.

➤ Ask participants to find partners and share their journal en-tries suggested by the "Spiritual Exercise" for Day 1 of this week. Each partner is to listen carefully to the other and repeat the priorities heard in those words. Encourage partners to identify any ways in which those "last words" shaped their words to others and their prayers this past week. Gather the group together. Allow any individuals or partners who may so wish to reflect on this exercise. Read aloud the quote from Shakespeare at the top of this week's Day 1 text, and suggest connections between it and what persons/partners may have shared in the priorities exercise above.

> *Lenten Emphasis:* The journey of Lent leads to the cross
> and to Jesus' final words and prayers. Affirm the power
> of "last words" to cast faith and priorities in sharp re-lief and of shaping prayer in Christ's example.

➤ Light the candle on the worship center table, inviting par-ticipants to pray in silence as they contemplate the figure on the crucifix or the symbol of the cross and the meaning of prayer offered from such a place.

➤ Lead the group in singing the first two verses of "The Gift of Love" ("Though I May Speak"). (See appendix.) Encourage participants to reflect as they sing on the role of love in defining the cross and its words and prayers.

INSIGHTS

➤ Invite participants to offer comments, share experiences, or raise questions stirred by this week's readings and daily exercises.

➤ Ask the participants to form groups of three or four. Suggest that they review their journal entries from the past week, relating a particular insight or experience from one of Jesus' cross prayers that will or already has shaped their own practice of prayer. Encourage conversation that explores reasons Jesus' cross prayers change our prayers.

> *Lenten Emphasis*: Stress the formation of our prayers in Christ's example on the cross, not just knowing the words he offered there but entering the spirit that evoked them. Encourage participants to exercise discernment in exploring the prayers of the cross that speak with particular power to them.

EXPLORATIONS

➤ Move the group, if possible, to your church's sanctuary. If not, ask the group to spread out in your meeting area. Reduce the lighting. Ask participants to visualize themselves keeping vigil by the cross. Explain that you will read (or play a recording of) the prayers of Jesus from the cross and that between each prayer there will be periods of silence or quiet instrumental music to encourage personal reflection. During the quiet times between prayers, participants may meditate upon each prayer of Jesus with these or similar questions in mind and heart: *What might the prayer have sounded and felt like to me in that place? What connection does the prayer have to my life? What does the prayer encourage me to pray?* Invite the participants to enter into the exercise by visualizing themselves taking their place beneath the cross. Carry out the reading or recordings (the prayers can follow the order of the scripture readings printed at the beginning of the Day 2 text, with the exception of Day 4's scripture). Allow several minutes between each of the cross prayers for adequate reflection time.

➤ Instruct the participants to form groups of three or four. Encourage conversations that reflect on this experience, particularly on the connections of Jesus' prayers to our lives and prayers. Allow participants to process emotional reactions to this experience as well. Return the group to your meeting area if you carried out this exercise in another part of the church.

> *Lenten Emphasis*: Lent journeys to and from the cross. Reflect with participants on ways the prayers at the cross go to the heart of what the entire Lenten journey has been about for you and for the participants.

➤ Read aloud Luke 23:46 (*Father, into your hands I commend my spirit*). Ask participants to study their hands and fingers and silently to reflect on how their hands have been used in this past week to create, to guide, to support, to show love. Reread Luke 23:46 and say these or similar words: **Imagine the hands of God held open. Entrust yourself to those hands. Place your joys, your struggles, your hopes, your faith in those hands. Feel yourself lifted up, supported, freed. Offer a prayer for the feelings you have at this moment, for the gift of being held in the hands of God.** Allow time for prayer.

Lenten Emphasis: Reflect on the entrusting of life into God's hands in Jesus' final words on the cross. Such trust need not happen only at life's final breath. Lent's journey, life's journey, invites us all along the way to entrust ourselves into God's hands.

CLOSING

➤ Gather participants around or in front of the worship center, and ask them to join hands. Invite those who so wish to respond to this session's activities, conversations, and prayers. Draw the session and study to a close by thanking participants for sharing this journey with you and with one another through the prayers of Jesus. Share something of what you will carry with you from this experience with prayer, and invite others who so wish to do the same.

Lenten Emphasis: Encourage participants to continue their vigil through any remaining Lenten services or programs at your church and to bring what they have experienced and learned of prayer through this study to those times.

➤ Sing the first and third verses of "The Gift of Love" ("Though I May Speak").

➤ Close with these or similar words: **The hands we hold connect us not only to the persons next to us but to this community of prayer we have formed during these past weeks. Just as we are held in one another's hands and prayers, so too are we held in the hands of God and in the continued prayers of Christ for us. Go in peace, knowing that love and grace hold you in Jesus Christ. . . . Go in prayer, having traveled the prayer paths of Christ's example. Shalom!**

APPENDIX

Songs for the Journey

⟨∼⟩

Can you imagine worship without music? Lyric and melody serve as conduits of the Spirit in ways that may escape our conscious awareness. Music touches emotion, summons memory, and reminds us of the beauty and mystery of standing in holy presence.

What follow are suggested songs for each of the sessions in this study. Depending on the traditions in your congregation, music may or may not be a typical component of study groups. I encourage you, however, to use these hymns to help set the context of each session, inviting participants to enter and leave each session's experience with the gift of music. You will need to find a song leader if you do not feel comfortable leading songs yourself. Indeed, asking for such help may even add another person to the group—or two, if an accompanist is needed. One option for the background music is to have a church musician record the songs so that participants can sing along to the recording.

If no one can be found to accompany or lead the music, simply read the lyrics in the form of litany. Do, however, try to involve music in the sessions. It will add variety to the experience for everyone. And for those among the participants for whom song lends itself to a spirit of worship and a sense of the holy, the music will hold the possibility of enabling even deeper connections with the session's themes.

Due to costs involved in reproducing copyrighted material, this appendix lists hymnal references for several of these songs.

Ask your pastor or church musician about access to copyrighted resources, and whether the congregation holds a license to copy such music for the purposes of these sessions.

SESSION 1—OUT OF SOLITUDE

Song: "Come and Find the Quiet Center"
Source: *The Faith We Sing* (Nashville, Tenn.: Abingdon Press, 2000), 2132.

SESSION 2—BY THE ROADSIDE

Song: "We Meet You, O Christ"
Source: *The United Methodist Hymnal* (Nashville, Tenn.: United Methodist Publishing House, 1989), 257.
The Presbyterian Hymnal (Louisville, Ky.: Westminster/John Knox Press, 1990), 311.

SESSION 3—ON THE MOUNTAINSIDE

Song: "Prayer Is the Soul's Sincere Desire"
Words by James Montgomery, 1818 (No copyright exists)
May be sung to the tune of "Amazing Grace" or "O for a Thousand Tongues to Sing"

O Thou, by whom we come to God,
the Life, the Truth, the Way:
the path of prayer thyself hast trod;
Lord, teach us how to pray!

SESSION 4—IN THE UPPER ROOM

Song: "When the Hour of Glory Beckoned" (based on John 17)
Words by John Indermark, Copyright 2002
Tune: HYFRYDOL (other possibilities: AUSTRIA, HYMN TO
JOY)

> When the hour of glory beckoned,
> Jesus lifted us in prayer;
> That Christ's joy be ours forever
> And God's unity we share.
> Called and sent by Christ, we witness
> To the love that makes all one.
> Christ, we ask your prayers raised for us
> Till God's realm is fully come.

> So does Christ still keep prayer's vigil
> For disciples, you and me;
> That the life that is eternal
> May in time the world might see.
> Jesus, like your prayers unceasing—
> Stir in us devoted hearts,
> That we may be always seeking
> How your presence to impart.

SESSION 5—AT THE GARDEN

Song: "Come Away with Me"
Source: *The Faith We Sing*, 2202.

SESSION 6—UPON THE CROSS

Song: "The Gift of Love" ("Though I May Speak")
Source: *The United Methodist Hymnal*, 408; *The Presbyterian
Hymnal*, 335.

OTHER BOOKS BY
JOHN INDERMARK

Neglected Voices
Biblical Spirituality in the Margins

The Bible features many voices of faith, including those whose lives are well-chronicled and those who are mere footnotes in biblical history. In *Neglected Voices*, Indermark explores the lives of lesser known biblical figures who have much to teach us about the importance of faithfulness in all places and times. (#891; separate leader's guide, #890)

Genesis of Grace
A Lenten Book of Days

Genesis of Grace leads us to a deeper understanding of God's grace by tracing it through the familiar stories of Genesis. Daily reflective readings explore the theme of God's forgiveness as revealed in such stories as the creation, the flood, Cain and Abel, and Abraham and Sarah. (#843; separate leader's guide, #844)

Setting the Christmas Stage
Readings for the Advent Season

Advent brings a rush of activities that often makes the pre-Christmas season lose its spiritual meaning. Using the device of a Christmas pageant to examine the biblical revelation, Indermark helps readers connect the biblical stories with their spiritual journeys. *Setting the Christmas Stage* helps readers refocus and thoughtfully consider the characters and places of the season as these impact the spiritual journey. (#947, leader's guide included)